Editor
Emily R. Smith M.A. Ed.

Editorial Project Manager
Elizabeth Morris, Ph.D.

Editor-in-Chief
Sharon Coan, M.S. Ed.

Illustrator
Howard Chaney

Cover Artist
Jamie Sochin

Art Coordinator
Denice Adorno

Imaging
Alfred Lau
James Edward Grace
Rosa C. See

Product Manager
Phil Garcia

Publisher
Mary D. Smith, M.S. Ed.

Web Hunts and Virtual Field Trips

Grades 3-5

Projects and Lesson Plans Using the Internet

Author

Deirdre Kelly

Teacher Created Resources, Inc.
6421 Industry Way
Westminster, CA 92683
www.teachercreated.com
ISBN: 978-1-57690-159-5

©2001 Teacher Created Resources, Inc.
Reprinted, 2008
Made in U.S.A.

The classroom teacher may reproduce copies of materials in this book for classroom use only. The reproduction of any part for an entire school or school system is strictly prohibited. No part of this publication may be transmitted, stored, or recorded in any form without written permission from the publisher.

Table of Contents

Introduction
    About This Book 4-5
    Online Research 6-7
    Internet Safety 8-9

Introduction to Web Hunts 10-11

Hunting for Mathematics
    Time 12-15
    Problem Solving 16-19
    Money 20-22
    Population 23-25

Hunting for Science
    Cloning 26-29
    Dinosaur Fossils 30-33
    Bridges 34-37
    Human Body 38-41

Hunting for Language Arts
    Words 42-45
    Storytelling 46-48
    Puppetry 49-51

Hunting for Social Studies
    People of Eminence 52-55
    U.S. History 56-59
    The 50 States 60-62
    Maps 63-65

Hunting for the Environment
    Take Action 66-69
    Endangered Animals 70-72
    Landforms 73-75

Table of Contents (cont.)

Introduction to Virtual Field Trips 76-77

Trips of Culture

    The Statue of Liberty.. 78-81

    Monet's Garden 82-84

    Baseball Hall of Fame... 85-87

Trips to the Water

    Oceans 88-91

    Coral Reefs 92-94

    The Everglades 95-97

Trips in Time

    Ancient Egypt 98-101

    The Freedom Trail.. 102-104

    The Renaissance 105-107

Trips in Space

    Solar System 108-111

    The Moon 112-114

    International Space Station 115-117

Trips to Nature

    Rain Forest.. 118-121

    Galapagos Islands 122-124

    The Desert 125-127

Trips to Famous Places

    Stonehenge.. 128-130

    Mount Rushmore 131-133

    The Great Wall of China 134-135

Appendix... 136-144

Introduction

About This Book

The Popularity of Hunts & Trips

Web hunts and virtual field trips are popular uses of the Internet in today's classrooms. There are many reasons for this popularity. First, hunts and trips make the most of the tool that is the Internet. They utilize the Internet's greatest gift – the storage of information. Second, hunts and trips help to advance valuable skills, including research skills, information management skills, and technological skills. Third, hunts and trips promote active learning. Too often we approach the Internet as a passive tool, like the television set. How great it is to have these two methods for becoming more active in our use of the Internet. It's time to use the Internet not just as an electronic encyclopedia but as a tool for constructive meaning.

Hunts vs Trips

The difference between Web hunts and virtual field trips is sometimes subtle. Generally, you create or employ a Web hunt to obtain information on a topic. Imagine the hunt mentality – searching, seeking, and tracking not prey, but information. The Web hunt can encompass any number of topics, but its intention is always the same – the exposure to or collection of information. You may want to create a Web hunt for your classroom topic of weather. Your learners use a collection of Web sites that you have gathered based on readability levels and content. At each site they review and collect information which they record in order to use the data in an offline activity or project. Some Web hunts require the collection of specific information; others are more open-ended and leave the question of which data should be collected to the learner.

Virtual field trips, on the other hand, are usually topic specific. They are centered around a geographic location or specific place of some kind. You may think that a Web hunt about a specific place might be called a virtual field trip, and you would be correct. But virtual field trips can be more than just the collection of information about a location – they often involve an open-ended exploration of the location. A virtual field trip to Greenland may take the form of close-ended questions to answer about Greenland, or it may be more inquiry-based, asking the learners to first explore Greenland via a collection of Web sites and then move offline to create a product which demonstrates their new knowledge.

How to Use this Book

This book is set up a bit differently than most with regards to the Web sites we've selected for use in our activities. Instead of publishing long, easily mistyped URLs, we've created a dynamic Web site to parallel the activities in this book. This new method is not only more convenient for you but also allows us to deal with the dynamic nature of the Internet. As the Internet grows and changes, Web sites come and go. If the Web site for one of our activities disappears or moves, we can easily replace it on the TCM Web site, making your new book last much longer than books where the URLs are less dynamic.

Introduction

About This Book (cont.)

How to Use this Book (cont.)

How does it work? It's simple! As you read through the book and come to activities you want to try with your learners, go to the *Teacher Created Resources* Web site for this publication:

http://www.teachercreated.com/books/2159

Then click on the corresponding links for that page in the book.

What You'll Find

This book is designed to do two things for you. First, it provides you with a collection of Web hunts and virtual field trips which encompass a variety of topics covered in most third-fifth grade classrooms. Secondly, the book is designed to help you advance your technology skills through exploration of Web hunts and virtual field trips–hopefully inspiring you to create your own. Use this publication as a supplement to your classroom curriculum.

Within this book you'll find two sections, one devoted to Web hunts and one devoted to virtual field trips. In each section you'll find content-based Internet activities. Each hunt or trip has teacher explanation pages followed by two or three reproducible student activity pages. The teacher pages provide you with brief background information, a listing of student learning objectives, the names and key questions or focus statements for each student activity, and Web site address information. The student pages provide the learners with the key questions and directions for each activity.

Grade Level Modifications

The activities within this book are designed for third to fifth graders. When you read through an activity which seems to be either too young or too old for your learners, we encourage you to make modifications. When making activities more appropriate for younger students, cut down on the number of objectives and focus on one or two which are most appropriate. Similarly, when advancing an activity, try to incorporate additional objectives which support your classroom learning in the same area of study. Creating a simpler or more complex version of the student activity page can alter many of the activities within this book. Try to focus on the parts of the existing activities that your learners can do, rather than the parts they cannot do.

A Word About Extensions and Closure

Occasionally, we included an extension idea or two, but because we wanted to fill this book with as many activities as possible, we opted to allow teachers to provide their own extensions and closures, since these areas often depend on the specific intentions of the teacher and needs of your learners. Providing closure on most of the activities requires nothing more than a collective debriefing of your learners. When the students finish the activity, take the time to come back together as a class to discuss their results.

Introduction

Online Research

Online research is an inexact art form rather than a precise science. When we consider the multitude of information available through the Internet, we must also consider the ramifications of such a collection on student research.

There are several schools of thought when considering online research for students. Of course, much of this depends on the age and ability levels of the students. While each individual situation should be considered, most schools feel safer with a blanket response or position. Let's take a look at the prevailing attitudes about online research for elementary students.

Willie-Nilly: Some teachers allow their students to go online to do research without any parameters at all. Sadly, this policy is usually a result of the teacher's lack of knowledge, rather than as a conscious statement about online research. These teachers often rely on the knowledge levels of their students, often greater than their own, to make the decisions for them. While many teachers wind up with this kind of Internet use, many others create this approach purposefully. They view open use of the Internet as a positive thing. They recognize the fact that Internet use has permeated our society, and they want their students to be well versed in its use without restrictions. These students are growing up in a world where they have access to the Internet almost everywhere.

Don't Go Near It: Other teachers and schools feel that because of the sheer amount of information that is "out there," it is developmentally inappropriate for elementary students to use any kind of search engine or tool. Teachers in this camp feel that it is their job to provide the students with a safe arena for their searches. As such, these teachers usually provide their students with small collections of three to six Web sites to use for each specific activity on which they're working. Generally, these teachers are not impressed with the hit-or-miss method of researching through search engines. They feel that it teaches better research skills when they provide the specific documents – documents they know contain the information the students need, documents they know to be accurate, documents which support rather than detract from the learning objectives.

In Between: There is, as for most situations in life, a happy middle ground – an in-between which borrows from each end of the spectrum to create another choice. Many teachers find themselves operating in this middle ground. With some activities, these teachers might provide specific Web sites to be used, while, with other projects they may allow their students to use kiddie search engines in order to train them in their use.

These teachers know that if the intent of going online is to collect information, their students should each have, at the bare minimum, a piece of paper and a pencil in hand when they go online. Better than this bare minimum, they know that their students need to have an activity specific note-taking form of some kind. We've provided you with an Internet Research Road Map (Appendix), which is designed to help students be more purposeful in their use of the Internet. These note-taking forms will help students to use their time more wisely.

Introduction

Online Research *(cont.)*

In Between *(cont.)*: Teachers in this middle ground know that their students need to be trained in the use of search engines. So many of the engines have distracting links, advertising, and extraneous information, it's very easy for students (especially those who are easily distracted) to be drawn away from their purpose. Students need to be shown what to ignore and what to focus on while they're researching. They need to know how to properly word an Internet search, a skill which baffles many adults, let alone elementary students. They need to have an understanding of the organization of the results which the search engines return. All of these needs can be met through simple practice. These teachers usually chose one or two kiddie engines to explore with their students, helping them become acclimated to the Internet environment.

Kiddie Search Engines

There are a variety of search engines which are designed for school-aged children. For a collection of kiddie search engines, go to *http://www.teachercreated.com/books/2159*. Click on page 7. Each one of these engines has specific details which you'll need to know about before taking children to them. We recommend that you go to these sites and literally play around on them. Do some searches of topics you're likely to ask your children to do. Get a feel for the return results. Look for organization and readability levels of the site. You know your learners best, so you'll be the best judge of which kiddie engines to use. The most important thing is that you feel comfortable with the process before taking your learners to it.

You might want to employ a few classroom procedures when using the search engines. Try these on for size:

- Have your students write their searching words on an index card and make sure they show it to you so that you can give them guidance and direction before they go online.

- Make a class rule that everyone pays attention to only the top three or four results. This can come in handy when the search engine brings back a list of hundreds!

- When you're first starting out, ask students to answer this question: How could I have made my search stronger? Keep a running list of answers on a poster in the room so that others can improve their skills too!

- Establish search partnerships which allow students to go online in pairs so that they can have two sets of eyes and two brains involved in their searching!

©Teacher Created Resources, Inc.   #2159 Web Hunts and Virtual Field Trips

Introduction

Internet Safety

Certainly one of the main concerns of the "online teacher" is Internet safety. By this point in time, most school systems have created some provision, policy, or statement of philosophy regarding student use of the Internet. Fueled by concerns from parents and occasional bad press, Internet use has gotten a bad rap in some areas. We'd like to address the issue of Internet safety in hopes of providing some guidance to teachers who might be just starting out and affirmation to those who have been traveling the information superhighway safely for years. Teachers should always provide both a purposeful use and appropriate supervision to their online activities.

Purposeful Use

How is the Internet approached in your classroom? Is it treated as a toy or a tool? There is a dangerous message being sent in classrooms where children are rewarded for completed work and good behavior with extra time to "play" on the Internet. In classrooms where the Internet is treated like the powerful tool that it is, there is a greater likelihood that the Internet will be used appropriately. The core of this debate about approaches is summed up in one little word: *intent*.

How is the Internet used in your classroom? When you ask your learners to go online to find out something about whales, you're setting them up for a frustrating experience – "I might find something, I might not." We wouldn't dream of standing a fourth grader at the doors to the New York Public Library and shoving him gently into the abyss, saying to him, "Run in there and find out something about whales." As teachers we wouldn't consider doing that. We'd go with him, guide him through the card catalog, bring him to the section on animals, point out the shelves where the whale books are, and help him find five books which might give him good information. We should treat the Internet the same way - telling our students to go to a class bookmarks page (a Web site collection of teacher-approved, content-specific sites) to find five facts about whales which we instruct them to write down on index cards. Then we've set them up for success!

Beyond the intent behind our use of the Internet is another word which comes in handy in this discussion: *direction*. It is imperative that we give our students a specific direction when they go online. They should go to some specific place and should do some specific thing when they get there. As we discussed in the section on online research, there is just too much information out there for students to manage alone. It is developmentally inappropriate to expect third, fourth, and fifth graders to be able to manage search results in excess of even 50 hits, let alone searches which bring back thousands of hits. Send your young students to a specific site or collection of sites which you've already approved. Be sure they know that they're expected to do something specific once they get there. Empower them with pre-printed Internet index cards. On one side print the word "Target" where they write the URL or page name of the Web site they're going to. The other side reads "Action" where they've written down what action they have to take once they have arrived at the site and read the content.

Internet Safety (cont.)

Appropriate Supervision

The second Golden Rule of Internet safety is providing appropriate supervision. Much of this will depend on your school's philosophy about Internet use. Most schools have a requirement that students have some kind of supervision while they're online. That supervision might be peer supervision or adult supervision. Adult supervision allows for greater accountability.

Of course, age also plays a part here. We have different concerns about Internet safety when working with high school students than we do when working with elementary students. The adult supervision for elementary school students often has more to do with helping them with the technology than it does with protecting them from harm's way. The location of the computers has a lot to do with providing supervision. If the computers are in your classroom, then you have greater control of the situation. Make sure the computers are positioned so that you can see the screens from anywhere in the room. If the computers are located elsewhere, in a lab or in the media center, then make arrangements to have a staff member from the media center or a parent volunteer provide supervision.

Class Expectations

When considering Internet safety, it's important to make sure that we recognize the importance of having clear expectations of our students regarding their use of the Internet. Let them know what kind of task commitment you require, let them know what kind of behavior is appropriate, and let them know what the consequences are if they don't meet those expectations. Most schools or school systems require students to sign an Acceptable Use Policy (AUP) which outlines appropriate use of the Internet. One thing to be sure of with an AUP is that you want to make sure that it is written on a level the students can understand, rather than in legalese which amounts to a signature without understanding. We've included a copy of an elementary-level AUP in the Appendix.

Time Constraints

One of the best strategies to use when you're attempting to ensure Internet safety is to place time constraints on your students' use of the Internet. If they know they have a limited amount of time to go online, they're more likely to use that time to accomplish their goals. Time constraints are often a naturally occurring factor, due to the ratio of students to computers, so this is a strategy which can be employed without much effort.

Filtering Software

Many school systems are using filtering software to help protect their children. The most important thing to consider here is that we should not allow the presence of a filtering program to lull us into a false sense of security. Filters or no, we should employ other safety strategies.

The bottom line with Internet Safety is this: If your students are trained to treat the Internet as a powerful tool, if they are supervised in their use, if they have specific purposes and objectives when they're online, and if they have a limited amount of time to be online, their online safety is much more secure.

Introduction to Web Hunts

On the following pages you will find hunts that span a variety of topics from math to social studies. Each of the hunts has a key question or focus point which helps your students to stay focused on their topic.

Key Questions and Statements

Hunting for Mathematics

What do we know about time?
How can we compare time measurements?
How would our lives be different if we didn't have any timekeepers?
Are there steps that can be used to solve ANY problem?
Is there always only one way to get to a right answer?
Explaining your thinking is an important part of problem solving.
Do we still barter today? What does bartering look like?
How is our money designed to protect from counterfeiting?
How fast are we growing?
How much does the U.S. population change in five minutes?

Hunting for Science

How does cloning work?
How do scientists decide what to clone?
What would life be like if we could clone people from the past?
Why is it important to discover, preserve, and display dinosaur fossils?
Does changing our perspective help us to understand things better?
How do scientists get dinosaur bones out of the earth?
What kinds of bridges are there, what are their shapes, and how do they work?
How does a bridge react when there is weight on it?
How does a bridge builder build bridges?
How can I keep all this information straight?
Are there any overlaps in the systems of the human body?
Do the systems of the human body remind us of things we see in the world around us?

Key Questions and Statements (cont.)

Hunting for Language Arts

How can I learn all about a Web site before I use it?
How does it feel to use impressive new words?
Are there patterns in languages (even make believe ones)?
How do I choose a good story?
How can I keep track of my story while I'm telling it?
Do I need special equipment and materials to make a puppet?
What techniques do real puppeteers use to make a good show?

Hunting for Social Studies

What similarities and differences are there among people of eminence?
Is there a difference between being "famous" and being "great"?
What would I have to do in order to become more like one of these people I admire?
How can the Revolutionary War be best represented on a time line?
What would it have been like to have been alive during the Revolutionary War?
Create a board game based on the events, places, and people of the Revolutionary War.
How can I decide which state is "the best"?
Create a commercial promoting one state over the others.
How many kinds of maps are there and what are they used for?
Mapmaking practice can be fun!

Hunting for Environment

What can I do to help save the environment?
How can I influence other people to do more to save the environment?
How can cities influence their environment?
What are the causes of extinction for certain animals?
Are there supporting causes which will help us to better understand the threats to our animal populations?
Can we show what we know about landforms through car creations?
Joining information and music can help me to remember cool stuff!

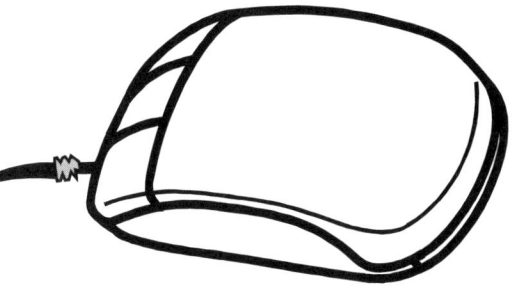

Hunting for Mathematics: Time

Time Marches On

Background

One of the marks of an advanced civilization is its mastery of time. Since the dawn of creation, time has been marching. From calendars to timekeepers, our attempts to measure it and even to harness it are benchmarks of our scientific and mathematical prowess. This hunt centers around our marking and measuring of time, how our measures evolved, and what they tell us about ourselves and our history.

Objectives

The student will explore the history of timekeeping.

The student will answer comprehension questions based on his or her readings.

The student will compare time measurements.

The student will consider his or her existence in a world with no timekeepers.

The student will construct cause and effect relationships.

The Hunt

Activity One: It's About Time!

Key Question: What do we know about time?

Activity Two: Measure for Measure

Key Question: How can we compare time measurements?

Activity Three: There's No Time Like the Present!

Key Question: How would our lives be different if we didn't have any timekeepers?

Focus Web Site

How Stuff Works: Time

Go to *http://www.teachercreated.com/books/2159*

Click on page 12, site 1

Companion Sites

Go to *http://www.teachercreated.com/books/2159*

A Walk Through Time	Click on page 12, site 2
Sundials	Click on page 12, site 3
World Time Zone Map	Click on page 12, site 4
Official Time	Click on page 12, site 5
How Stuff Works: Pendulum Clocks	Click on page 12, site 6

Hunting for Mathematics: Time

It's About Time

http://www.teachercreated.com/books/2159   Click on page 12, site 1

Key Question: What do we know about time?

Directions: Use the *Measuring Time* chart on the Web site above to explore these questions and find their answers.

1. List eight measurements of time which are used on this Web site:

   _____, _____, _____, _____,

   _____, _____, _____, _____

2. After reading the information on this Web site, create your own definition of the word time: _____

3. How old is planet Earth? _____

4. How long have dinosaurs been extinct? _____

5. What civilization created the first known clock? Hint: It's called a "sundial"!

   _____

6. How many minutes are there in a day? _____

7. What is the smallest increment of time we use on a regular basis? _____

8. Is a "time zone" a natural or a man-made tool? _____

9. What is the purpose of time zones? _____

   _____

10. Is "Daylight Savings Time" a natural or a man-made tool? _____

11. What is the origin of "Daylight Savings Time"? _____

    _____

12. What planets did the Romans use to name the days of the week?

    _____, _____, _____, _____,

    _____, _____, _____

13. How long is a year, really? _____

14. Would your birthdays be closer together or farther apart if we measured a year the "right way"? Why? _____

Hunting for Mathematics: Time

Measure for Measure

http://www.teachercreated.com/books/2159   Click on page 12, site 1

Key Question: How can we compare time measurements?

Directions: Using the *Measuring Time* chart on the How Stuff Works Web site, figure out the equations below. You may want to work in teams since it's helpful to have a partner keep track of counting and recording! We've left you some space, so be sure to show your work–even if it's tally marks and drawings!

1. How many "blinks of an eye" does it take you to tie your shoe? _____
   Show your work:

2. How many "blinks of an eye" does it take you to dial your phone number? _____
   Show your work:

3. How many "heartbeats" are there in one "long commercial"? _____
   Show your work:

4. How many "heartbeats" does it take you to sharpen a new pencil? _____
   Show your work:

5. How many "long commercials" does it take you to walk from one end of the hallway to the other? _____
   Show your work:

6. How many decades are in a "typical human life span"? _____
   Show your work:

7. How many "typical work days" are there in one day? _____
   Show your work:

#2159 Web Hunts and Virtual Field Trips ©Teacher Created Resources, Inc.

Hunting for Mathematics: Time

There's No Time Like the Present!

http://www.teachercreated.com/books/2159   Click on page 12, site 1

Key Question: How would our lives be different if we didn't have timekeepers like clocks, watches, calendars, etc?

Directions: Timekeepers, like watches, clocks, and calendars, help us to keep track of our lives. After exploring the How Stuff Works Web site, complete the graphic organizer below by creating if–then statements like this one: "If we lived in a world with no timekeepers, then how would we know when to get up in the morning?" Then try to think of solutions to the statements to complete the final column.

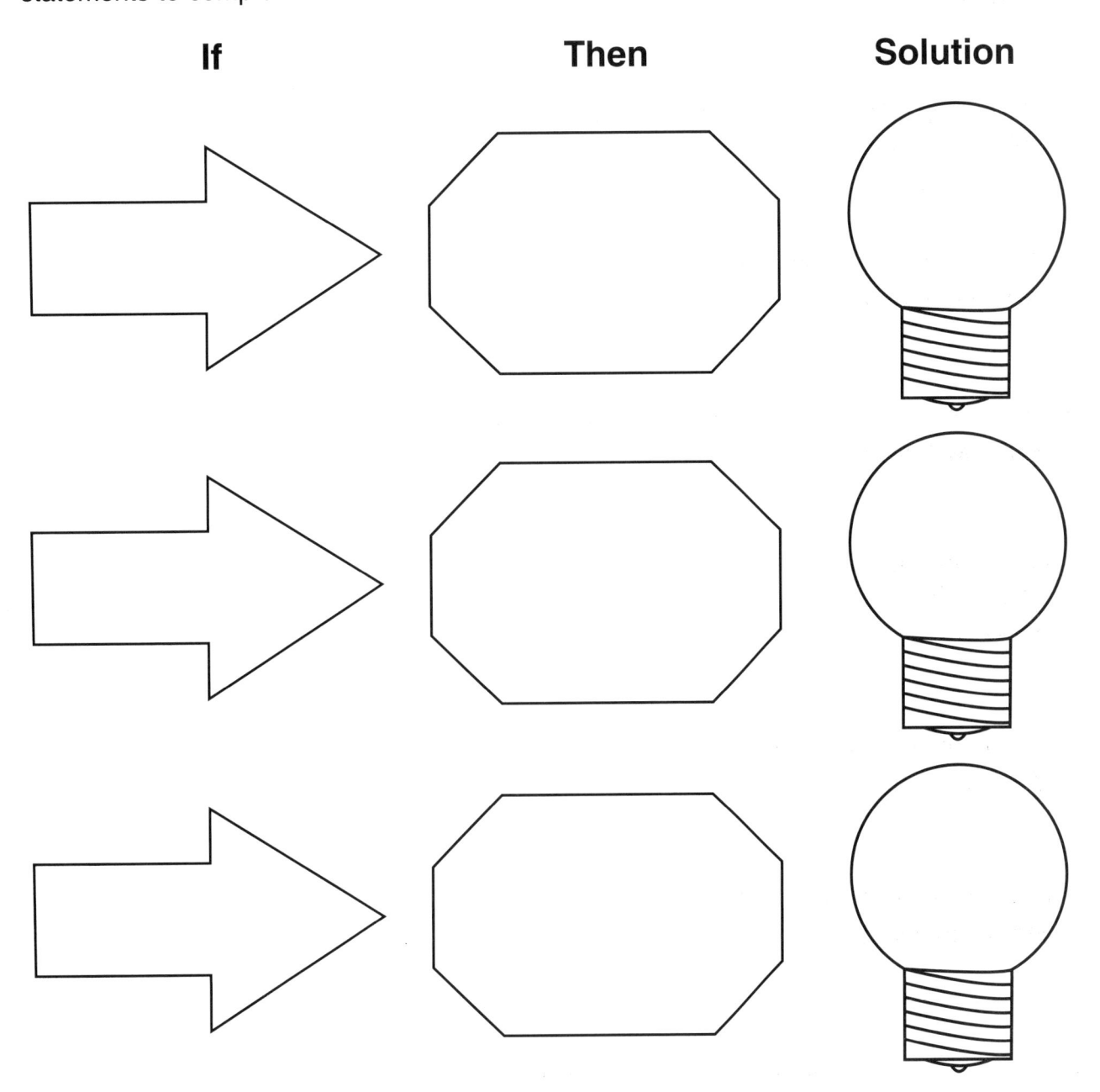

If　　　　　　　**Then**　　　　　　　**Solution**

©Teacher Created Resources, Inc.　　　　15　　　　#2159 *Web Hunts and Virtual Field Trips*

Hunting for Mathematics: Problem Solving

Figure It Out!

Background

A skilled problem solver is an asset to his or her community, company, and self. Teaching students how to solve problems is one of the most valuable sets of skills we can instill in our students. Because of its algorithmic nature, mathematics offers a rich training ground for the exploration and development of problem-solving skills. In this mathematics hunt, we will ask you to travel to several sites to expose your students to interesting and unique problem-solving opportunities.

Objectives

The student will employ a four-step, problem-solving process.

The student will explore and recognize a variety of problem-solving strategies.

The student will recognize that diversity of thought is a mathematical strength.

The student will participate in metacognition (thinking about his/her own thinking) while solving a problem.

The Hunt

Activity One: Step by Step
  Key Question: Are there steps that can be used to solve any problem?

Activity Two: There's More Than One Way to Eat an Apple!
  Key Question: Is there always only one way to get to a right answer?

Activity Three: Tell Me a Story
  Key Statement: Explaining your thinking is an important part of problem solving.

Focus Web Site

Figure This!

   Go to *http://www.teachercreated.com/books/2159*

   Click on page 16, site 1

Companion Sites

   Go to *http://www.teachercreated.com/books/2159*

Mathletics	Click on page 16, site 2
Your Party	Click on page 16, site 3
So, You're Planning a Trip?	Click on page 16, site 4

Hunting for Mathematics: Problem Solving

Step by Step

http://www.teachercreated.com/books/2159   Click on page 16, site 1

Key Question: Are there steps that can be used to solve ANY problem?

Directions: Use this problem-solving blueprint to solve a problem of your choice from the *Take a Challenge* section of the Figure This! Web site.

Step One: Find the problem

Many problems have extra information in them (sometimes it's put there just to confuse you!). The very first step in solving a problem is making sure you can find the real problem! Read through the problem you've selected and write **just** the problem here.

Step Two: Plan the problem

Any time you solve a problem, it's always best to think out a plan before actually working on the problem. Take some "think time" right now to consider your options – are you going to need to add or maybe multiply? Will you need to get a ruler or another tool to solve this problem? Have you seen a problem like this one before?

Take a moment to write down some of your thoughts about your problem.

Step Three: Work the problem

This is where the planning pays off – solving the problem. Use your math skills and do as you would if you had a twelve-foot ice cream sundae in front of you – dive in and keep going until it's all gone! Be sure to show your work.

Step Four: Check the problem

You've probably done the problem correctly, but it's always a good idea to check your work to make sure your fingers actually did what your brain told them to do! Take a moment now to go back and check your work.

Hunting for Mathematics: Problem Solving

There's More Than One Way to Eat an Apple!

http://www.teachercreated.com/books/2159   Click on page 16, site 1

Key Question: Is there always only one way to get to a right answer?

Directions: Put slips of paper, numbered one through nineteen in a paper bag. Have someone from your class pull a slip out of the paper bag. Go to the *Take a Challenge!* section of the Figure This! Web site to find the challenge that matches the slip pulled from the bag. Solve the selected problem on this page. Once everyone is finished, get into small groups of five or six students to share the solutions and the strategies you used in your "Workshop Area." After sharing solutions and talking about how each person solved the problem, organize the problem-solving papers into categories to show similar strategies. For example, you might want to create a pile of papers where the person drew a picture to solve the problem, or you might want to a make a pile of papers where the solver built a chart or graph.

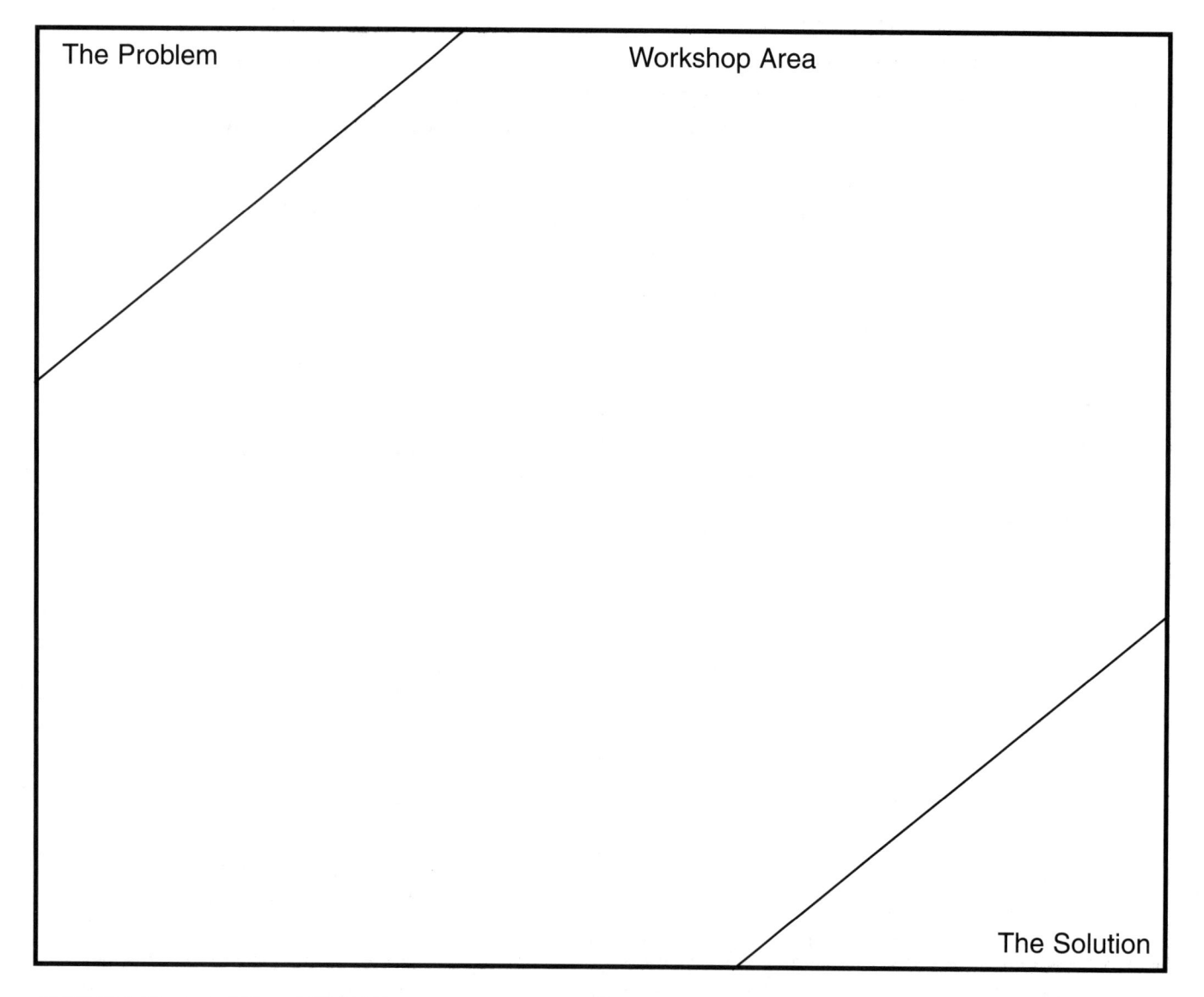

| The Problem | Workshop Area |

The Solution

Hunting for Mathematics: Problem Solving

Tell Me a Story

http://www.teachercreated.com/books/2159   Click on page 16, site 1

Key Statement: Explaining your thinking is an important part of problem solving.

Problem solving isn't just about getting to the right answer; it's also about understanding the journey to the right answers.

Directions: Choose any problem from the *Take a Challenge!* section of the Figure This! Web site. Once you've selected your problem, use the left side of this page to solve the problem as you usually would. After you've done that, complete the right side by telling the story of what you were thinking while your mind solved the problem. You may have just added or multiplied to solve the problem, but your brain probably did more than just that; it probably remembered a problem like this one that you've solved before. Perhaps it organized the information in the problem into sections before starting to solve it, or perhaps you started solving the problem but then realized you were doing it wrong and began again.

What My Hand Did	What My Head Did

Hunting for Mathematics: Money

Dollars and Sense

Background

Money is so commonly used and is such an easy way to buy and sell goods that it is hard to imagine that there was a time when money was not used, a time when money was brand new. Today money seems to run the world, and there may be a time in the not-so-distant future when money will change so completely that perhaps we won't even have currency anymore, just tallies on an electronic financial scorecard. The history of money is an interesting trip down memory lane, a history not just of the way we transact business but of ourselves, of the maturity of our civilization. Our children are likely to learn that four quarters make a dollar; but there is more to money than just the equations; there is the story it can tell.

Objectives

The student will explore the historical aspects of money as it relates to our growth as a civilization.

The student will participate in a simulated barter society in order to better understand the effectiveness and operations of a barter economy.

The student will explore the safety features incorporated into the making of U.S. currency.

The students will complete a "Know, Learned, Use" chart based on the anatomy of money.

The Hunt

Activity One: Let's Make a Deal!
Key Question: Do we still barter today? What does bartering look like?

Activity Two: Smart Money
Key Question: How is our money designed to protect from counterfeiting?

Focus Web Sites

NOVA Online: The History of Money
Go to *http://www.teachercreated.com/books/2159*
Click on page 20, site 1

The Anatomy of a Bill
Go to *http://www.teachercreated.com/books/2159*
Click on page 20, site 2

Companion Sites

Go to *http://www.teachercreated.com/books/2159*

The History of Money	Click on page 20, site 3
Circulation of Money	Click on page 20, site 4

Hunting for Mathematics: Money

Let's Make a Deal!

http://www.teachercreated.com/books/2159   Click on page 20, site 1

Key Question: Do we still barter today? What does bartering look like?

Directions: After reading about bartering on the History of Money Web site, participate in the following simulation.

1. Lay three items on top of your desk which are valuable to you.
2. Put your name on each item so that you can get it back once the exercise is over.
3. Fill out the first two columns of the chart below about your items.
4. Participate in a bartering session with the class for 15 minutes.
5. Complete the rest of the chart (see example) and the questions beneath it.

Item for Trade Cost	What it would take to give this up	What I ended up trading it for	Profit, Loss, or Draw ?
horse key chain $2.50	a lot of stuff-I love this horse key chain.	compass $2.00	lost 50 cents

So, what kind of barterer are you (circle one)?   Awesome   OK   Need Practice

On the back, answer these questions: How can you judge who is a good barterer?
Name five kinds of bartering that you do regularly.

©Teacher Created Resources, Inc.   #2159 Web Hunts and Virtual Field Trips

Hunting for Mathematics: Money

Smart Money

http://www.teachercreated.com/books/2159   Click on page 20, site 2

Key Question: How is our money designed to protect from counterfeiting?

Directions: Read the Anatomy of a Bill Web site and then complete the chart below.

Five Things I Already Know About How Money is Made

▲
▲
▲
▲
▲

Five Things I Learned About How Money is Made

❏
❏
❏
❏
❏

Five Things I Can Do With My New Knowledge

✳
✳
✳
✳
✳

Hunting for Mathematics: Population

Gee, It's Crowded in Here

Background

In this Age of Information, we must equip our students with information management skills which will help them to become better problem solvers and mathematicians. Studies of our population give students an almost unlimited supply of dynamic raw data to use while learning information management skills. In addition, working with population statistics and figures helps students gain a new understanding of their place in an ever-changing world. In this hunt your students will have the opportunity to collect and analyze raw data. The activity sheets provided aid your students in collecting and organizing their data. Once completed, these data sheets should serve as the ingredients of class discussions and comparisons.

Objectives

The student will record, analyze, and interpret raw data.

The student will use graphic organizers to manage raw data.

The student will compare large numbers in a meaningful context.

The student will organize information in order to draw conclusions.

The student will explore the nature of population accounting.

The student will participate in recordkeeping based on a dynamic subject.

The Hunt

Activity One: Look! There's Another One!
  Key Question: How fast are we growing?

Activity Two: Five Minutes in America
  Key Question: How much does the U.S. population change in five minutes?

Focus Web Site

Census Bureau Population Clocks

  Go to *http://www.teachercreated.com/books/2159*

Click on page 23, site 1

Companion Sites

  Go to *http://www.teachercreated.com/books/2159*

Population Map	Click on page 23, site 2
Population Map 2	Click on page 23, site 3
Population Growth	Click on page 23, site 4

Hunting for Mathematics: Population

Look, There's Another One!

http://www.teachercreated.com/books/2159   Click on page 23, site 1

Key Question: How fast are we growing?

Directions: Spend one week collecting information on either the world or U.S. populations from the U.S. Census Bureau Web site (the main page, don't click into either of the clocks – yet!). Take readings at the beginning and the end of each the day. Be consistent, choose a morning and afternoon time that's convenient and then stick to them. Record your data in the chart below. Then construct a bar or line graph to share your data. Feel free to choose either the U.S. or world population, or if you're feeling adventurous, do both!

Morning Reading Time: _____   Afternoon Reading Time: _____

	Morning Reading	Afternoon Reading	Increase
Monday			
Tuesday			
Wednesday			
Thursday			
Friday			

Try This: After Tuesday afternoon's reading, estimate what you think Friday afternoon's population will be!

Use the empty graph below to create a bar or line graph of the data in your chart!

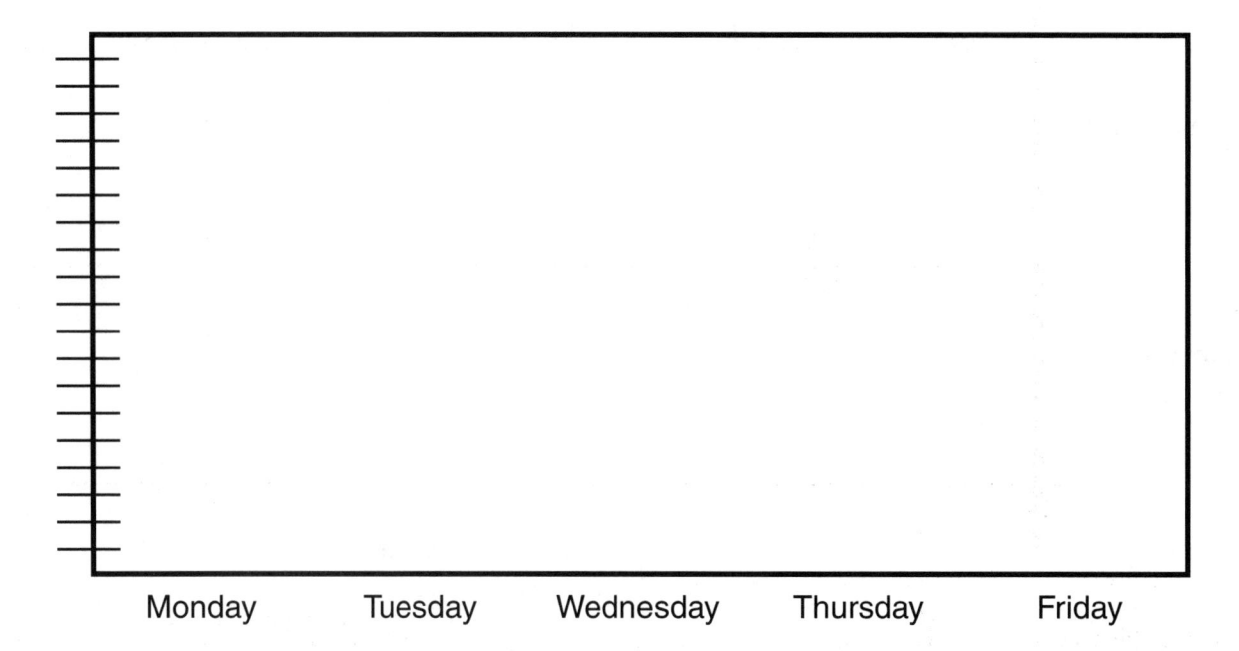

Monday   Tuesday   Wednesday   Thursday   Friday

#2159 Web Hunts and Virtual Field Trips   24   ©Teacher Created Resources, Inc.

Hunting for Mathematics: Population

Five Minutes in America

http://www.teachercreated.com/books/2159   Click on page 23, site 1

Key Question: How much does the U.S. population change in five minutes?

Directions: From the U.S. Census Bureau Population Clock Web site, click on the blue box around the U.S. population. Use the information on this site to complete the time line of U.S. population for the next five minutes. Don't forget that you need to click on the Reload/Refresh button every minute.

Start Time: _____

	Births	Deaths	Newcomers	Homecomings
First Minute				
Second Minute				
Third Minute				
Fourth Minute				
Fifth Minute				

Stop Time: _____

Totals: Births: _____   Deaths: _____   Newcomers: _____   Homecomings: _____

©Teacher Created Resources, Inc.   #2159 Web Hunts and Virtual Field Trips

Hunting for Science: Cloning

Two of a Kind

Background

At the close of the 20th century, an international spotlight was aimed at the science of cloning, all because of a cute little bundle of wool named "Dolly." This reach into what was once discussed only in science fiction novels gave the international community quite a bit to think about, from organ transplants, to cloning our favorite pets, to human cloning. This rich and current topic is a wonderful example to our students of real-world science – its power, its effects, and its possibilities for the future. Though the scientific details behind cloning are a bit complicated for some elementary students, the ideas and possibilities surrounding it are rich with opportunities for learning. A brief study of cloning would be a wonderful extension after a study of human reproduction. All that focus on eggs and genes and the fantasy implications for cloning can take some of the nervousness out of a sometimes intense topic.

Objectives

The student will appreciate an elementary understanding of cloning.

The student will appreciate and weigh the strengths and weaknesses of him/herself and his/her peers.

The student will create a visual representation of personality characteristics.

The student will appreciate and weigh the qualities of people from history.

The Hunt

Activity One: Quit Cloning Around: This Is Serious Science
   Key Question: How does cloning work?
   Note: This activity requires an understanding of the terminology and the concepts of reproduction.

Activity Two: A Little of This and a Little of That
   Key Question: How do scientists decide what to clone?

Activity Three: A Blast from the Past
   Key Question: What would life be like if we could clone people from the past?

Focus Web Site

The Why Files?: Cloning

   Go to *http://www.teachercreated.com/books/2159*

   Click on page 26, site 1

Companion Sites

   Go to *http://www.teachercreated.com/books/2159*

   I can do that!: Cloning   Click on page 26, site 2

   I can do that!: Genes   Click on page 26, site 3

Hunting for Science: Cloning

Quit Cloning Around: This Is Serious Science

http://www.teachercreated.com/books/2159 Click on page 26, site 1

Key Question: How does cloning work?

Directions: After reading the cloning instructions on The Why Files? Web site, break down the process of cloning into five steps and fill out the step-by-step graphic organizer below to explain how cloning works.

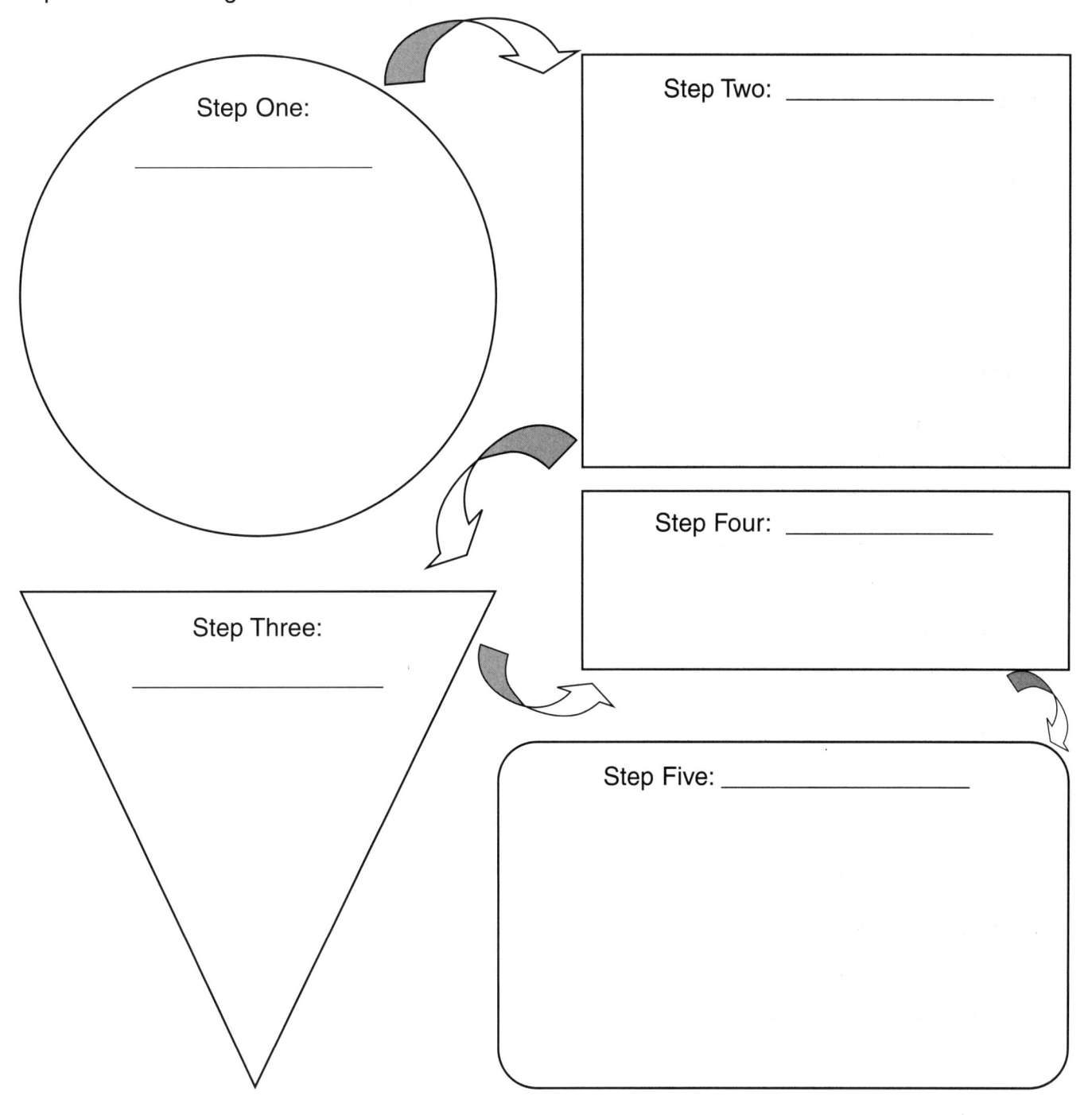

Step One: _____

Step Two: _____

Step Three: _____

Step Four: _____

Step Five: _____

©Teacher Created Resources, Inc.   #2159 Web Hunts and Virtual Field Trips

Hunting for Science: Cloning

Name: _____ Date: _____

A Little of This and A Little of That

Key Question: How do scientists decide what to clone?

Directions: Pretend that you are a scientist in a cloning laboratory. One day you're daydreaming a little in your office, and you glance up at a picture of yourself and your four best friends from a trip to the zoo last year. You start thinking about how great all of your friends are and how they each have special qualities that make them unique. Then you start thinking about what good qualities you would want to save from each of your friends in a test tube to put in the deep freeze and use it one day to make the world a better place. Label the test tubes below with the names of four friends. Then fill the test tube with each friend's best quality. Be creative in the color and design of the quality! (Maybe the quality of "Easy Laughter" has smiley faces in it, or maybe "Helpfulness" has helping hands floating around inside!)

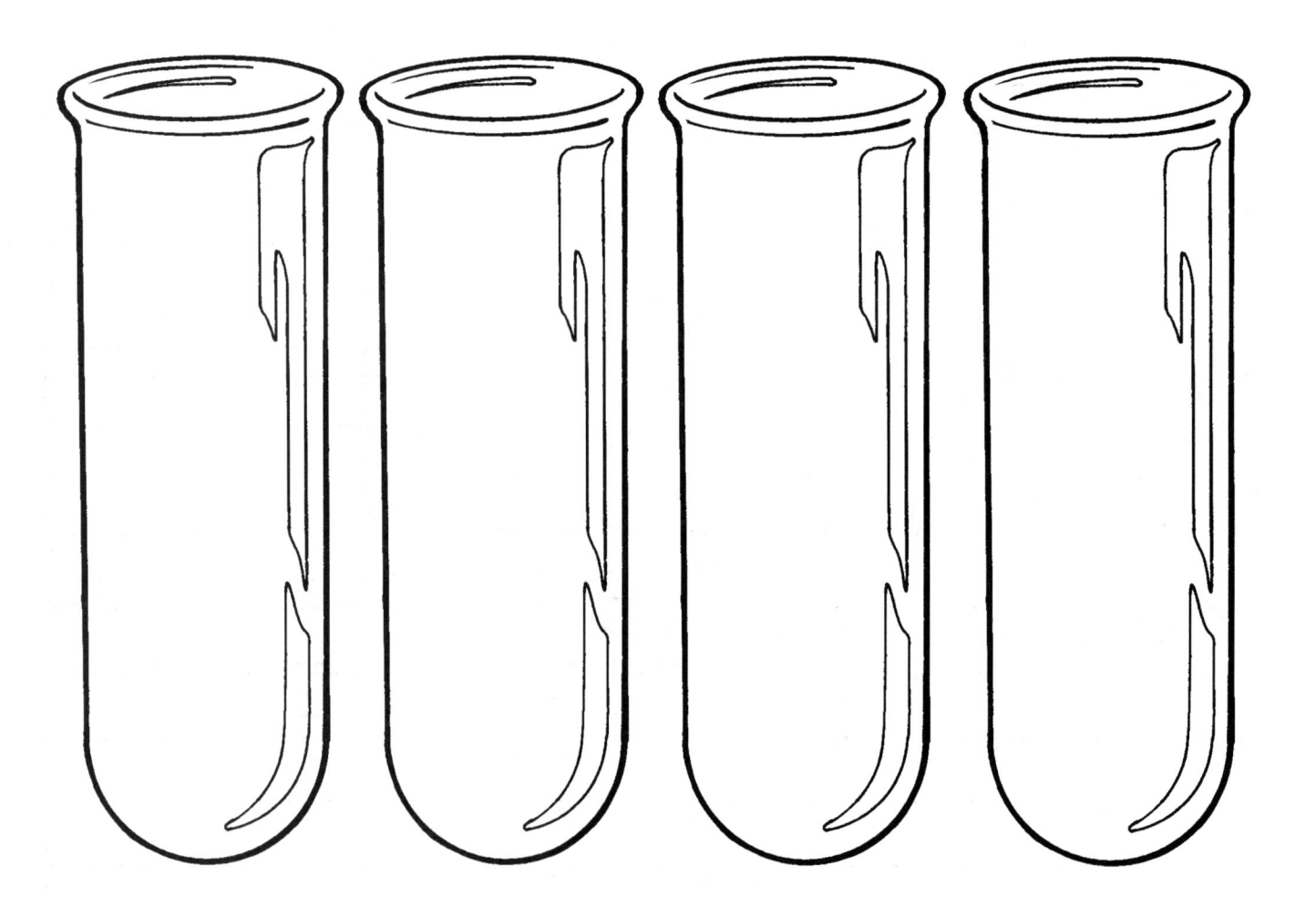

If you have the time, you might want to think about your own special qualities. What would YOUR test tube be filled with?

Hunting for Science: Cloning

Name: _____ Date: _____

A Blast from the Past

Key Question: What would life be like if we could clone people from the past?

Directions: In the picture frame below, draw a picture of the person you would like to create if you could piece him or her together, using the personality qualities and physical features of people from history. Your portrait can show physical features of the people of the past, but you'll need to use the side boxes to show what personality traits you'll give to your new person. When you're done, use the chart below to show whose genes you used, which trait you chose and why!

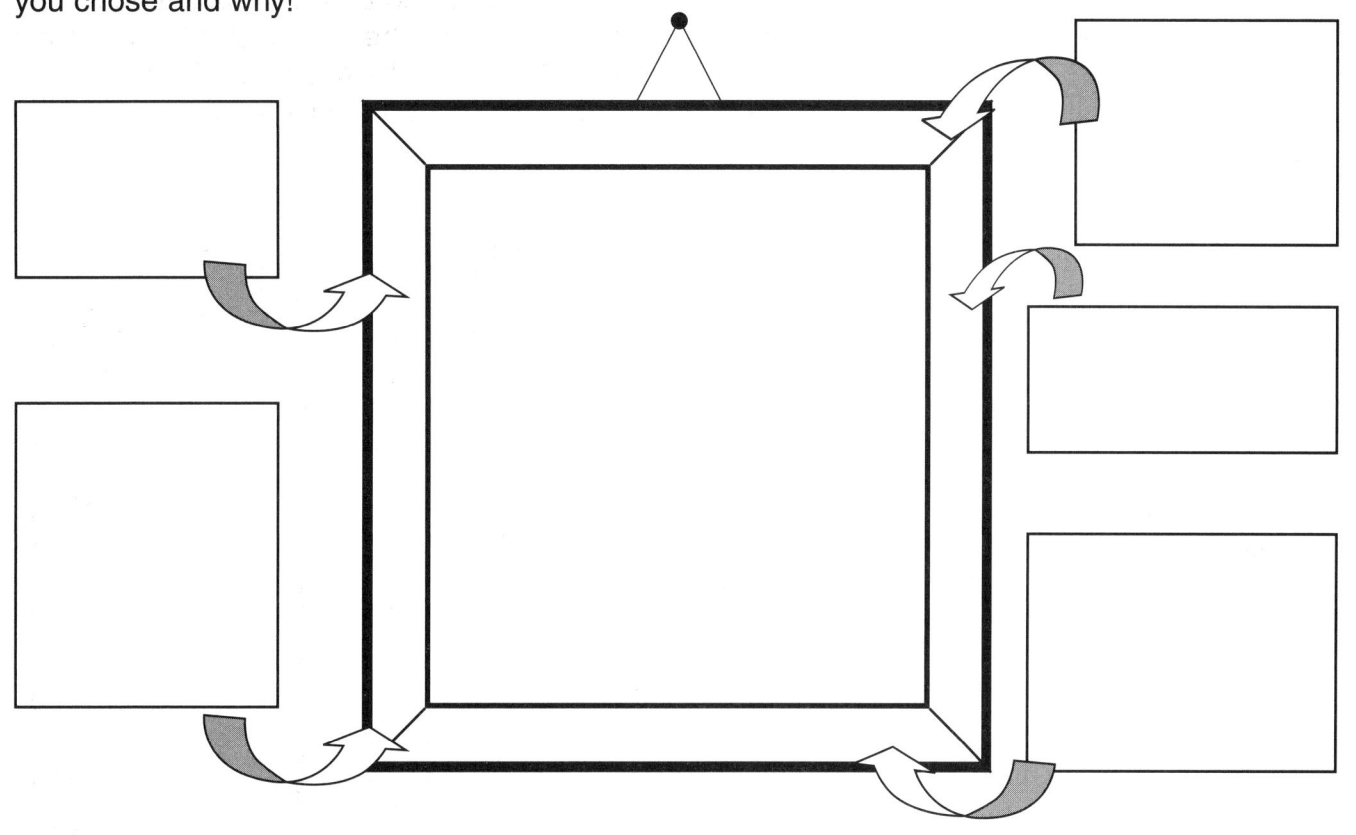

Person from the Past	What I Used from Him/Her	Why

©Teacher Created Resources, Inc.   29   #2159 Web Hunts and Virtual Field Trips

Hunting for Science: Dinosaur Fossils

Them Bones, Them Bones

Background

The discovery of and ensuing fight for the bones of a 90% intact Tyrannosaurus rex fossil captured the imaginations of thousands. The story of the discovery, the battle, and the final homecoming of these bones has been brought to a personal level because the bones have a story to tell and a name to go along with them – Sue. The Field Museum has done an excellent job of providing a behind-the-scenes view of the process a fossil goes through in order to become a main attraction on a museum floor. This hunt will allow your students to adopt different perspectives, that of the fossil and that of the scientist, while learning new information about dinosaurs and fossils.

Objectives

The student will explore writing on a specific topic from a variety of perspectives.

The student will employ persuasive writing and narrative writing styles.

The student will use a writer's planning tool to plan a written work.

The student will employ note-taking skills to obtain information from a Web site.

The Hunt

Activity One: Dear Sir or Madam:
   Key Question: Why is it important to discover, preserve, and display dinosaur fossils?

Activity Two: You Be Sue!
   Key Question: Does changing our perspective help us to understand things better?

Activity Three: Journaling with Sue
   Key Question: How do scientists get dinosaur bones out of the earth?

Focus Web Site

Sue at the Field Museum

   Go to *http://www.teachercreated.com/books/2159*

   Click on page 30, site 1

Companion Sites

   Go to *http://www.teachercreated.com/books/2159*

The Why Files?: Going, Going, Gone	Click on page 30, site 2
Enchanted Forest: Dinosaur Fossils	Click on page 30, site 3
Dinosaur Floor	Click on page 30, site 4
Fossils	Click on page 30, site 5

Hunting for Science: Dinosaur Fossils

Dear Sir or Madam:

http://www.teachercreated.com/books/2159   Click on page 30, site 1

Key Question: Why is it important to discover, preserve, and display dinosaur fossils?

Directions: Pretend that you are the curator of a museum. Your department has just heard about an incredible find in South Dakota – a T. rex fossil which is 90% complete. You know that this would be a wonderful addition to the museum's growing paleontology department, but you also know that it will take millions of dollars to buy the remains. Write a letter to the heads of several multimillion dollar corporations to ask them to give you the money you need to buy Sue. Use the section of the Sue Web site called *What's New with Sue* to help you convince the company presidents that this is a worthy cause.

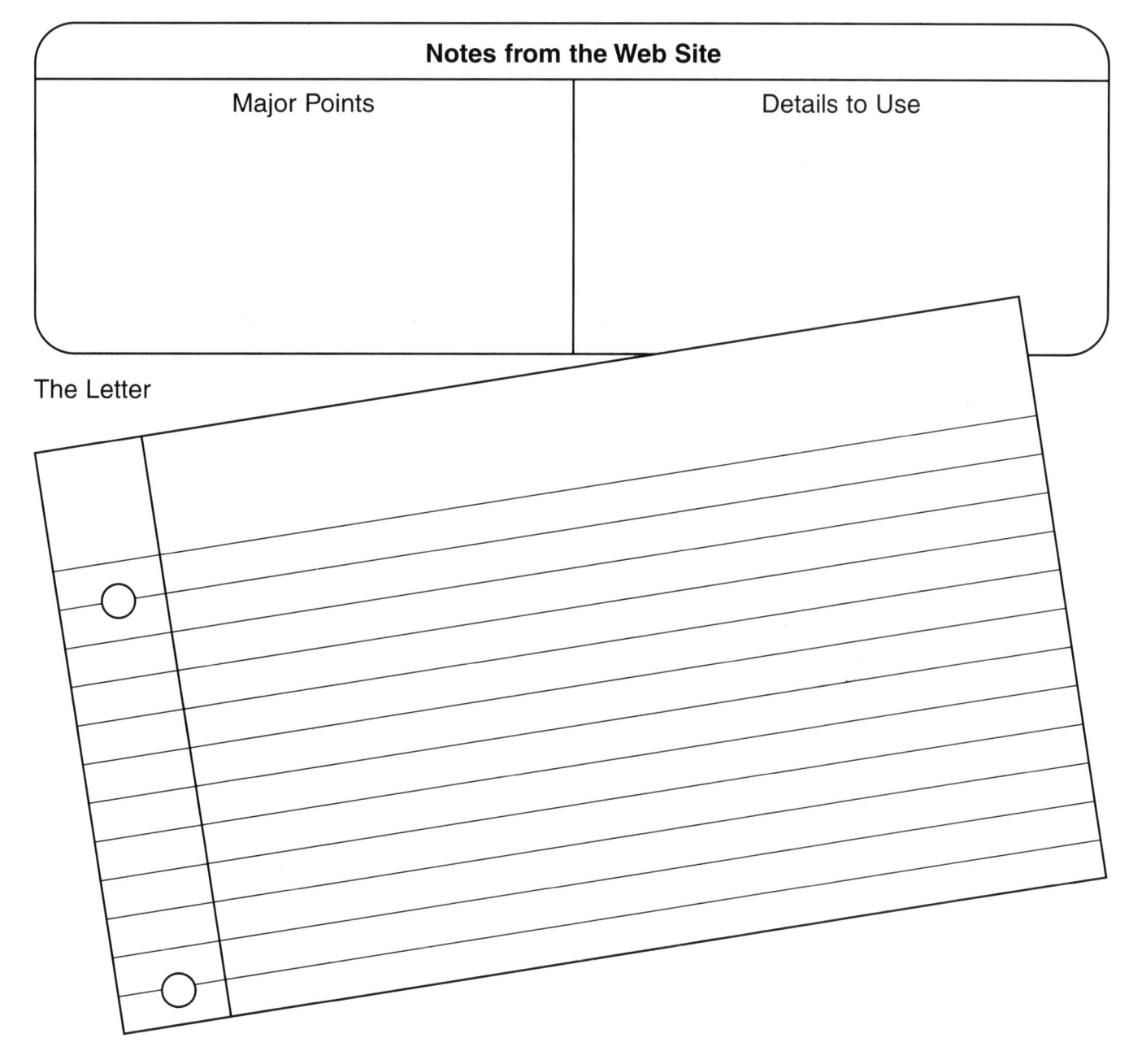

Notes from the Web Site	
Major Points	Details to Use

The Letter

Hunting for Science: Dinosaur Fossils

You Be Sue!

http://www.teachercreated.com/books/2159   Click on page 30, sites 1-2

Key Question: Does changing our perspective help us to understand things better?

Directions: In this activity you get to be Sue! Hopefully you've explored Sue's story on the Sue Web site (and maybe even learned a little bit more on The Why Files? Web site). Now it's time to put yourself in her shoes, er… claws. Use the space below to make a Writer's Plan which you'll use to help you write a creative story (on your own paper). Your purpose is to tell Sue's story from her perspective. There's a ton of information on the Web sites, so you may want to choose a certain area of Sue's life to explore, either her life while she was alive (the life of a T. rex), what happened when and after she died (becoming a fossil), the discovery and collection of her bones (from the ground to the stage), or you might even project into the future and tell her story as the world's most famous T. rex on display in a museum!

A Writer's Plan

My perspective:

I'm telling this story from Sue's perspective by putting myself in her place.

What part of Sue's story am I going to tell?

_____

Facts from the Web site I need to be sure to include:

Notes to myself to help me stay on track for each part of my story:

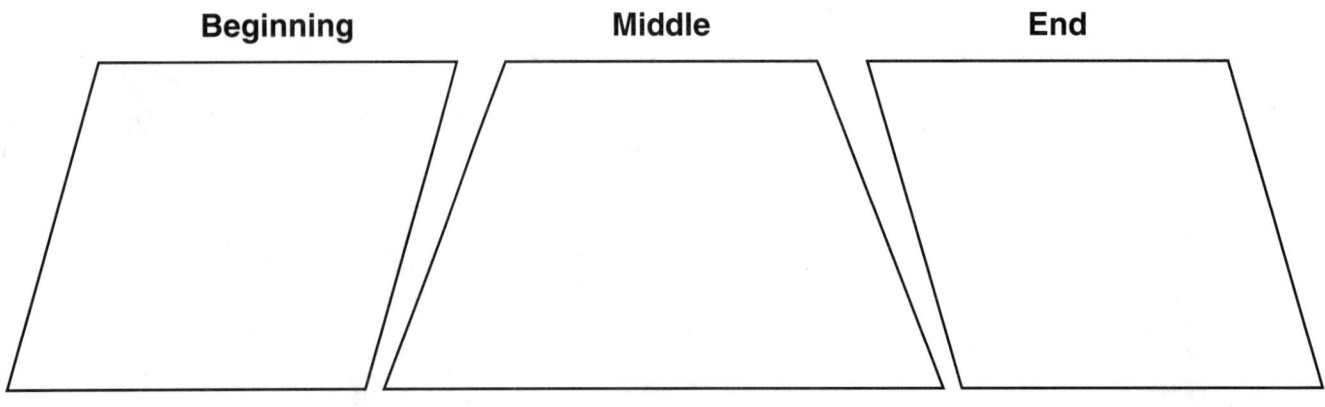

Beginning	Middle	End

Hunting for Science: Dinosaur Fossils

Journaling with Sue

http://www.teachercreated.com/books/2159   Click on page 30, site 1

Key Question: How do scientists get dinosaur bones out of the earth?

Directions: On the Sue Web site, go to the *Preparation and Mounting* section and then find the step-by-step process of how scientists get the dinosaur fossils out of rock. Read that section carefully and study the pictures. Once you are familiar with the process, complete the following journal entries as if you were the lead scientist in charge of processing Sue's bones.

Journal Entry: Day One

Today was incredible! When I walked into the lab, there was a huge pile of crates and boxes all full of the fossils of Sue the T. rex! We're waiting for a few more boxes to get here tomorrow, so we can't start opening the plaster casts until then. I can't wait! I'll have to get the tools ready today and find a few helpers to lend a hand.

Journal Entry: Day Two – opening the field jackets

_____

_____

_____

Journal Entry: Day Three – rock removal

_____

_____

_____

Journal Entry: Day Four – more rock removal

_____

_____

_____

Journal Entry: Day Five – fine tools

_____

_____

_____

Journal Entry: Day Six – the air abrasion room

_____

_____

_____

©Teacher Created Resources, Inc.   #2159 Web Hunts and Virtual Field Trips

Hunting for Science: Bridges

Bridges

Background

Bridges are worthy of study for a variety of reasons: their familiarity, their beauty, and their strength. In this hunt, students will learn more about the main types of bridges through online research and through hands-on activities.

Objectives

The student will use a note-taking form to record detailed information.
The student will explore the relationship between compression and tension.
The student will participate in a pre-study estimate and verification process.
The student will demonstrate and express in writing critical thinking skills used in a decision-making process.
The student will develop a construction plan for a building project.
The student will construct a simulated bridge out of common materials.

The Hunt

Activity One: An Abridged Version of Bridges
  Key Question: What kinds of bridges are there, what are their shapes, and how do they work?

Activity Two: Bridges in Action
  Key Question: How does a bridge react when there is weight on it?
  Materials: red and blue pencils, markers, or crayons

Activity Three: ACME Bridge Builders
  Key Question: How does a bridge builder build bridges?
  Materials: Have a collection of a variety of bridge building materials: spaghetti, lasagna, angel hair pasta, mini-marshmallows, graham crackers, Saltines, rubber bands, brads, paper clips, paper towel and toilet paper rolls, toothpicks, shish kebab skewers, etc.

Focus Web Site

NOVA Online: Build a Bridge

  Go to *http://www.teachercreated.com/books/2159*

  Click on page 34, site 1

Companion Sites

  Go to *http://www.teachercreated.com/books/2159*

  Click on page 34 —

Bridges	site 2	Bridges Collection	site 5
Brooklyn Bridge	site 3	Bridges	site 6
Brooklyn Bridge History	site 4	How Stuff Works: Bridges	site 7

Hunting for Science: Bridges

An Abridged Version of Bridges

http://www.teachercreated.com/books/2159   Click on page 34, site 1

Key Question: What kinds of bridges are there, what are their shapes, and how do they work?

Directions: While you carefully read the NOVA Build a Bridge Web site, use the chart below as a note-taking guide to help you record information from the site. You'll want to keep track of four pieces of information: the name of the bridge, its shape, how it works, and at least one actual bridge of that type.

If you're feeling adventurous, take the challenge and play the Build a Bridge game (Step 3).

Bridge Name	Shape of Bridge	How It Works	Actual Example

©Teacher Created Resources, Inc.   35   #2159 Web Hunts and Virtual Field Trips

Hunting for Science: Bridges

Bridges in Action

http://www.teachercreated.com/books/2159 Click on page 34, site 7

Key Question: How does a bridge react when there is weight on it?

Directions:

1. Go to the site called How Stuff Work: Bridges and read *only* the section of the site titled *The Basics*.

2. Complete the left-hand side of this activity sheet based on what you think might be correct according to your knowledge of bridges.

3. Then go back and read the rest of the site to see if you were correct! Be sure to take notes while you're reading so that you can compare your guesses to the actual answers!

NOTES

Bridges are designed to react to two main forces: compression and tension. As weight is added to a bridge, the relationship between the compression and tension changes. Compression acts to shorten an object and tension acts to lengthen an object. The best example of this is an ordinary spring. When you pinch two ends of a spring together you are exerting compression on it and when you pull its ends away from each other, you are exerting tension on it.

What I Think	What I Know

#2159 Web Hunts and Virtual Field Trips © Teacher Created Resources, Inc.

Hunting for Science: Bridges

ACME Bridge Builders: Thinking & Planning Sheet

http://www.teachercreated.com/books/2159   Click on page 34, site 1

Key Question: How does a bridge builder build bridges?

Directions: Using the materials your teacher provides for you, construct one of the bridges you learned about on the NOVA Build a Bridge Web site. It will be up to you to make decisions about your building materials. You should choose your materials carefully, because some materials will not work in certain bridge types. Your bridge will be tested by your teacher who will carefully lay as many pennies as possible in the center of the bridge, to see how much weight it can hold. Use this sheet as your "Thinking and Planning Sheet." Just like real bridge builders, you can make all the mistakes you want to – on paper. Just make sure you make them all before you start building! Be sure to make changes to your plan as you encounter problems in the "field."

Type of Bridge: _____

Selected Building Materials	Reason for Choosing Them

The Building Plan

Hunting for Science: Human Body

Everybody Has a Body

Background

The human body is a complex organism, and some people devote their entire lifetimes to its exploration and understanding. While we don't have that much time, we do have enough time to become more familiar with some of the major systems of the body. This hunt is designed to give students a better understanding of the systems and magic of the human organism.

Objectives

The student will select important data from a Web site source.

The student will evaluate, prioritize, and organize information.

The student will compare and contrast systems of the human body.

The student will seek out natural and man-made patterns in the world around him/her.

The student will draw correlations between new information and the world around him/her.

The Hunt

Activity One: Information Overload!
  Key Question: How can I keep all this information straight?
  Materials: index cards

Activity Two: Any Overlaps?
  Key Question: Are there any overlaps in the systems of the human body?

Activity Three: Silly Me, It's a Simile!
  Key Question: Do the systems of the human body remind us of things we see in the world around us?

Focus Web Site

A Look Inside the Human Body

  Go to *http://www.teachercreated.com/books/2159*

Click on page 38, site 1

Companion Site

  Go to *http://www.teachercreated.com/books/2159*

Human Anatomy Online   Click on page 38, site 2

Hunting for Science: Human Body

Information Overload!

http://www.teachercreated.com/books/2159   Click on page 38, site 1

Key Question: How can I keep all this information straight?

Directions: First, read through the information on the Human Body Web site. Once you're familiar with the site, get a stack of twelve index cards from your teacher. On the top of three cards, write Skeletal System. On the top of another set of three cards, write Circulatory System. Continue until you have three cards for each system. With your cards in hand, go back to the Web site for some detail hunting. Your objective is to narrow the amount of information you have to deal with by choosing what you think are the three most important facts about each system. You may write only one fact on each card, so there won't be a mountain of information on each card, just a simple fact. Once your whole class is finished, it's time to combine the cards into a group set. A good way to do this is to have one or two people handle each set of cards (Circulatory, Skeletal, etc.). Those in charge of the cards should eliminate any duplicate cards in the pile, leaving only those cards that the members of your class think are the most important pieces of information about each system. Once you've walked through this process, use the chart below to keep a record of the class findings (you might want to put a star next to your personal favorites).

The Body Systems	What's Most Important

©Teacher Created Resources, Inc.   #2159 Web Hunts and Virtual Field Trips

Hunting for Science: Human Body

Any Overlaps?

http://www.teachercreated.com/books/2159   Click on page 38, site 1

Key Question: Are there any overlaps in the systems of the human body?

Directions: After reading through the Human Body Web site, go back to the site with this organizer in hand and see what you can turn up for each section of these Venn diagrams. It's up to you to choose which body systems you're going to put in each circle. Some combinations will be tougher than others, so choose wisely! If you're feeling like a bigger challenge, try making a Venn diagram with four circles!

Don't forget to label your circles!

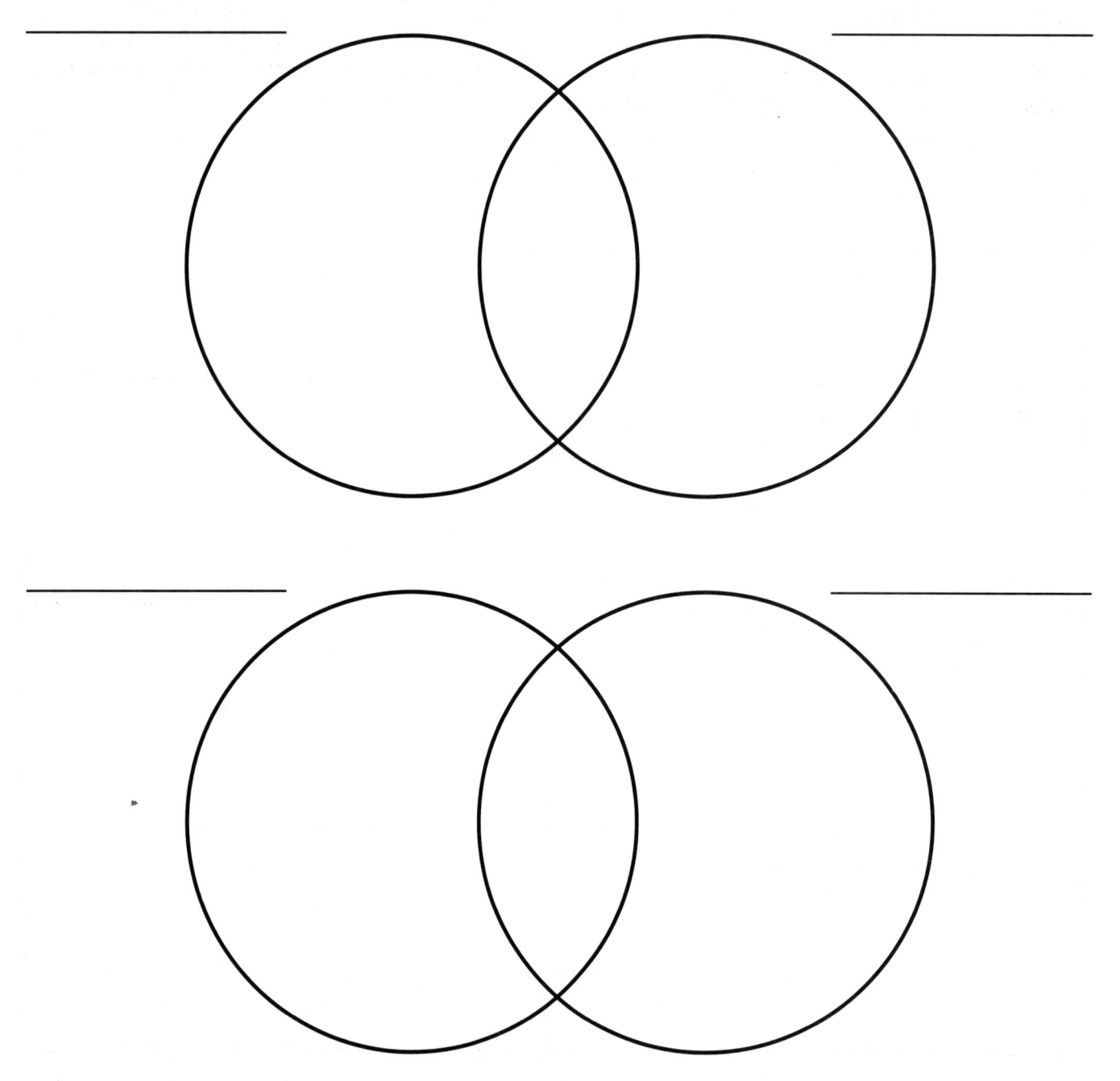

_____   _____

_____   _____

Hunting for Science: Human Body

Silly Me, It's a Simile!

http://www.teachercreated.com/books/2159   Click on page 38, site 1

Key Question: Do the systems of the human body remind us of things we see in the world around us?

Directions: After becoming knowledgeable about the four body systems represented on the Human Body Web site, read the paragraph below and then work with a partner to complete the activity.

One of the wonderful things about the natural world is its tendency to repeat itself. Where a monkey has success in using anchored vines for transportation, a spider has equal success in using anchored webs for lodging. Where there is a system of veins to move blood through the body, there is also a system of veins we call rivers to move water through the landmasses. There are other examples of both natural and man-made systems that mimic our human body systems; your job is to recognize them and explain your comparisons.

The skeletal system is like . . .
The respiratory system is like . . .
The circulatory system is like . . .
The digestive system is like . . .

©Teacher Created Resources, Inc.   #2159 Web Hunts and Virtual Field Trips

Hunting for Language Arts: Words

Wordy, Wordy

Background

We use words all the time – in our writing, in our conversations, even in our thinking! This Language Arts Hunt centers around one of our favorite things–words. In this hunt students will explore Word Central, a site created by *Merriam Webster®* the dictionary people.

Objectives

The student will create a site map of a multi-layered Web site.

The student will determine the personal value of a Web site.

The student will advance his/her vocabulary.

The student will apply new vocabulary in real-world conversational context.

The student will identify patterns in a written code.

The student will create a language code of his/her own.

The Hunt

Activity One: Site Mapping
  Key Question: How can I learn all about a Web site before I use it?

Activity Two: Go Ahead, Try It On!
  Key Question: How does it feel to use impressive new words?

Activity Three: Secret Codes Inc.
  Key Question: Are there patterns in languages (even make-believe ones)?

Focus Web Site

Word Central

Go to *http://www.teachercreated.com/books/2159*

Click on page 42, site 1

Companion Sites

Go to *http://www.teachercreated.com/books/2159*

Journal Topics	Click on page 42, site 2
Short Subject Topics	Click on page 42, site 3

Hunting for Language Arts: Words

Site Mapping

http://www.teachercreated.com/books/2159   Click on page 42, site 1

Sometimes, when you're traveling around in cyberspace, you bump into a Web site that has a whole bunch of information on it or a collection of things to do on the site. As a good Web hunter, you'll need to know how to get the "lay of the land" before using a Web site. This activity will help you to explore any Web site thoroughly.

Key Question: How can I learn all about a Web site before I use it?

Directions: Use this activity sheet to help you get to know the Word Central Web site. We've started you off in the right direction; you take it from there!

Page Name	Places to Go from Here	Things to Do on This Page	Come Back Here?
Build Your Own Dictionary	Daily Buzzword Games For Educators	submit a word read latest entries browse alphabetically search dictionary	definitely - it's cool!

©Teacher Created Resources, Inc.   #2159 Web Hunts and Virtual Field Trips

Hunting for Language Arts: Words

Go Ahead, Try It On!

http://www.teachercreated.com/books/2159   Click on page 42, site 1

Learning new words is such a cool thing to do – it makes your writing so much more interesting and your conversations more lively. The trick is that most people are too shy to use a new word because they're afraid that they'll sound goofy or that they might use the word incorrectly. In this activity you won't have to be afraid of sounding silly, because everyone will be doing it right along with you! In fact, you get points for using new words – the newer the better!

Key Question: How does it feel to use impressive new words?

Directions: Use the *Cafeteria and Cafeteria's Archive* on the Word Central Web site to decide on seven words that you're going to use in a conversation with a group of friends. Make them new and interesting or outrageously unknown words; it's up to you! Write them down on the left side of this activity sheet. Write down the definition too so that you're sure that you're using the word correctly in the conversation. Your teacher will give you a topic to discuss as a group. Begin the conversation as you would any other conversation with your friends. When you see an opportunity to use one of your cool new words, use it! As you use each word, check it off on your list. Your teacher will be listening to make sure that you've used the words correctly. You'll get points for using a unique word and more points for using the word correctly. You'll also get *bonus points* if you can work the definition of the word you use into the conversation so that the other people in your group will learn what the word means too! On the right side of this sheet, you can keep track of the cool new words that other people in your group use so that you can learn about them, too!

My Words	Definitions	Used	Other People's Words
			My Conversation Points

Hunting for Language Arts: Words

Secret Codes, Inc.

http://www.teachercreated.com/books/2159   Click on page 42, site 1

Key Question: Are there patterns in languages (even make-believe ones)?

Directions: Think of a short, simple phrase to use for this activity. Something uncomplicated is going to work best (The dog ran past the car.). Once you've created your phrase, go to the Word Central Web site and visit the second floor *Science and Computer Labs* to perform the word experiments on your phrase. Study what happens to your phrase so that you can decipher the codes and experiments. Once you've cracked the codes, fill in the chart below. If you have the time, create a code of your own and try it out on some of your classmates and their phrases!

Phrase: _____

	Code Name	How the Code Works
Science Lab	Vowel Monster	
	Space Jumble	
	Pocatenate	
	Morse Code	
Computer Lab	Secret Cipher	
	File Flipper	
	Vowel Changer	
	My Code	

©Teacher Created Resources, Inc.   #2159 Web Hunts and Virtual Field Trips

Hunting for Language Arts: Storytelling

Tall Tales

Background

Storytelling has been around since man first learned how to communicate. We tell stories in so many different media these days–in television, in movies, on audiotapes, on laserdiscs– it's easy to let the simplest and most elegant form of storytelling slip by unnoticed–oral storytelling. Being an effective storyteller requires a synthesis of many skills, from public speaking, to reading an audience, to effective use of language, to understanding the context of written expression.

Objectives

The student will evaluate a story's qualities for storytelling use.

The student will recognize the strengths and weaknesses of written language.

The student will identify the main parts of a story.

The student will create a graphic organizer to aid in storytelling.

The Hunt

Activity One: Choosing a Story to Tell
Key Question: How do I choose a good story?

Activity Two: Storyboard
Key Question: How can I keep track of my story while I'm telling it?

Focus Web Site

Tales of Wonder

Go to *http://www.teachercreated.com/books/2159*

Click on page 46, site 1

Companion Sites

Go to *http://www.teachercreated.com/books/2159*

Tips for Storytellers 1	Click on page 46, site 2
Tips for Storytellers 2	Click on page 46, site 3
Tips for Storytellers 3	Click on page 46, site 4

Hunting for Language Arts: Storytelling

Choosing a Story to Tell

http://www.teachercreated.com/books/2159   Click on page 46, site 1

Great storytelling must begin with a great story. However, choosing the perfect story from the limitless stories available in books, on Web sites, and even in your own mind can be a tough job! When choosing a great story, make sure it's one you will enjoy telling. This activity is going to help you discover what kinds of stories you will like the best.

Key Question: How do I choose a good story?

Directions: Find a story on the Tales of Wonder Web site and read it. If you think you might like to use that story for a storytelling, try completing these story questions to help you make your decision. If you wind up with more "yeses" than "nos," then you've got yourself a story!

The Title of the Story: _____

Story Questions	Yes	No
1. Does this story happen in an interesting or exciting place? (i.e. outer space, underwater, underground, or on a mountain top)		
2. Does this story happen in an interesting or exciting time? (i.e. in the past or future, in dinosaur times or ancient Egypt)		
3. Does this story have a small number of characters? (Too many characters can make the story confusing and hard to tell.)		
4. Does this story have interesting characters? Any cool accents you could use? Any funny, silly, or goofy characters?		
5. Does this story have interesting, funny, or compelling events? Is there a mystery or a problem to solve in the story? Is there any cool action that takes place?		
6. Does this story remind you of any other stories you know?		
7. Does this story capture your interest?		
8. Does this story remind you of your life at all?		
9. Does this story have a good "lesson" at the end?		
Will this story make a good storytelling story?		

Hunting for Language Arts: Storytelling

Storyboard

http://www.teachercreated.com/books/2159   Click on page 46, site 1

Key Question: How can I keep track of my story while I'm telling it?

Directions: Use this activity sheet to help you to organize your story in large "chunks" or pieces so that you will not leave out any parts while you're telling your story. Break your story into five main parts: The Beginning, The First Big Event, The Second Big Event, The End, and The Moral. If you get stuck on any part of the story, just use this sheet for a reminder of where to go next!

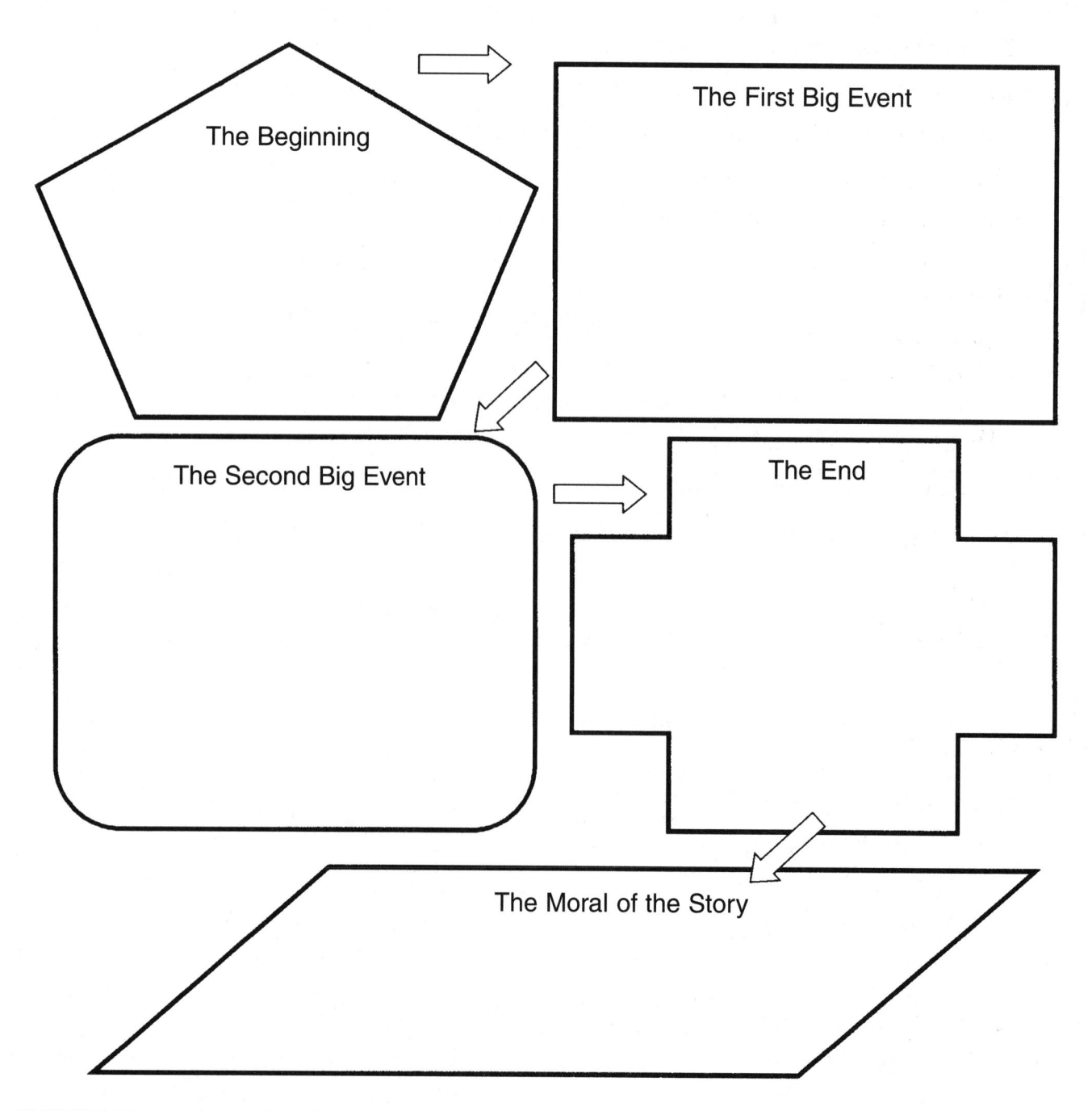

The Beginning

The First Big Event

The Second Big Event

The End

The Moral of the Story

Hunting for Language Arts: Puppetry

You Are the Puppet Master

Background

Puppetry is an age-old and much adored form of communication and entertainment that enjoys an active following to this day. Creating puppets and making them come alive through skits and stories is a great way for your students to experience language development. In this hunt your learners will be encouraged to study suggestions and ideas from other puppet makers in order to construct a scrap puppet of their own. Additionally, your students will study and collect professional puppetry strategies and tips that they will use to create a quality puppet show of their very own.

Objectives

The student will create a scrap puppet for use in a skit/play/show.

The student will incorporate outside ideas/suggestions with his/her own ideas.

The student will collect and organize information from a Web site.

The student will evaluate a personal performance in order to find improvements.

The student will apply professional techniques to an amateur production.

The Hunt

Activity One: Create A Puppet
   Key Question: Do I need special equipment and materials to make a puppet?

Activity Two: Puppeteering Like a Pro!
   Key Question: What techniques do real puppeteers use to make a good show?

Focus Web Site

Puppets

   Go to *http://www.teachercreated.com/books/2159*

   Click on page 49, site 1

Companion Sites

   Go to *http://www.teachercreated.com/books/2159*

History of Puppets	Click on page 49, site 2
The Puppet Gallery	Click on page 49, site 3
Tips for Readers' Groups	Click on page 49, site 4

Use these to create your very own puppet production:

Plays from Aaron Shepard	Click on page 49, site 5
Stories from Aaron Shepard	Click on page 49, site 6

Hunting for Language Arts: Puppetry

Create-A-Puppet

http://www.teachercreated.com/books/2159   Click on page 49, site 1

Key Question: Do you need special equipment and materials to make a puppet?

Directions: Go to the Web site and click on the *Scrap Puppets* button to learn more about making scrap puppets. Use this activity page to help organize your ideas so that you can make the best scrap puppet ever!

Ideas I got from the page	Ideas floating around in my head

Materials I'm going to collect	A picture of my design

Now—go and make your puppet!

Hunting for Language Arts: Puppetry

Puppeteering Like a Pro!

http://www.teachercreated.com/books/2159   Click on page 49, sites 1-4

Key Question: What techniques do real puppeteers use to make a good show?

Directions: Use the Web sites above to help you to fill out this activity page. Write down at least three tips in each section. Keep it handy during your practices for your first puppet show, and you're sure to be a hit!

Tips for Before the Show

1.
2.
3.

Tips for During the Show

1.
2.
3.

Tips for After the Show

1.
2.
3.

After the show is over, you might want to write down some tips you'll want to use next time!

Tips for Next Time

©Teacher Created Resources, Inc. #2159 Web Hunts and Virtual Field Trips

Hunting for Social Studies: People of Eminence

I Want to Be Just Like You!

Background

Through a study of people of eminence, our students come to a closer relationship with history because much of it can be appreciated on a more personal level than when it is studied through dates and battles and events. Attaching a face and a name to a movement or period in history and experiencing that individual's struggle can promote new levels of understanding.

Objectives

The student will explore biographical information to gain new knowledge about people of eminence.

The student will compare and contrast people of eminence.

The student will recognize the differences between being great and being famous.

The student will identify a personality whom he/she would most like to emulate.

The student will participate in a self-examination in order to set goals which will bring him/her closer to recognizing a personal improvement goal.

The Hunt

Activity One: Compare and Contrast

Key Question: What similarities and differences are there among people of eminence?

Activity Two: Famous or Great?

Key Question: Is there a difference between being "famous" and being "great"?

Activity Three: From Here to There

Key Question: What would I have to do in order to become more like one of these people I admire?

Focus Web Site

Time: Heroes and Icons

Go to *http://www.teachercreated.com/books/2159*

Click on page 52, site 1

Companion Sites

Go to *http://www.teachercreated.com/books/2159*

People Who Made A Difference in American History	Click on page 52, site 2
Women of the Hall	Click on page 52, site 3
Their Stamp on History	Click on page 52, site 4
Meet Amazing Americans	Click on page 52, site 5
Biographies of the Founding Fathers	Click on page 52, site 6

Hunting for Social Studies: People of Eminence

Compare and Contrast

http://www.teachercreated.com/books/2159   Click on page 52, site 1

Key Question: What similarities and differences are there among people of eminence?

Directions: Use the Time: Heroes and Icons Web site to study a few famous people. Once you've read about a handful of people, choose two who captured your interest. You might want to read about these two people once more and take a few notes this time, just to make sure you've collected all the information you need. You could even check out a few of the companion sites to see if there is any more information on the people you've selected. After your information gathering is done, fill in the Venn diagram below to help you compare and contrast the people you have selected.

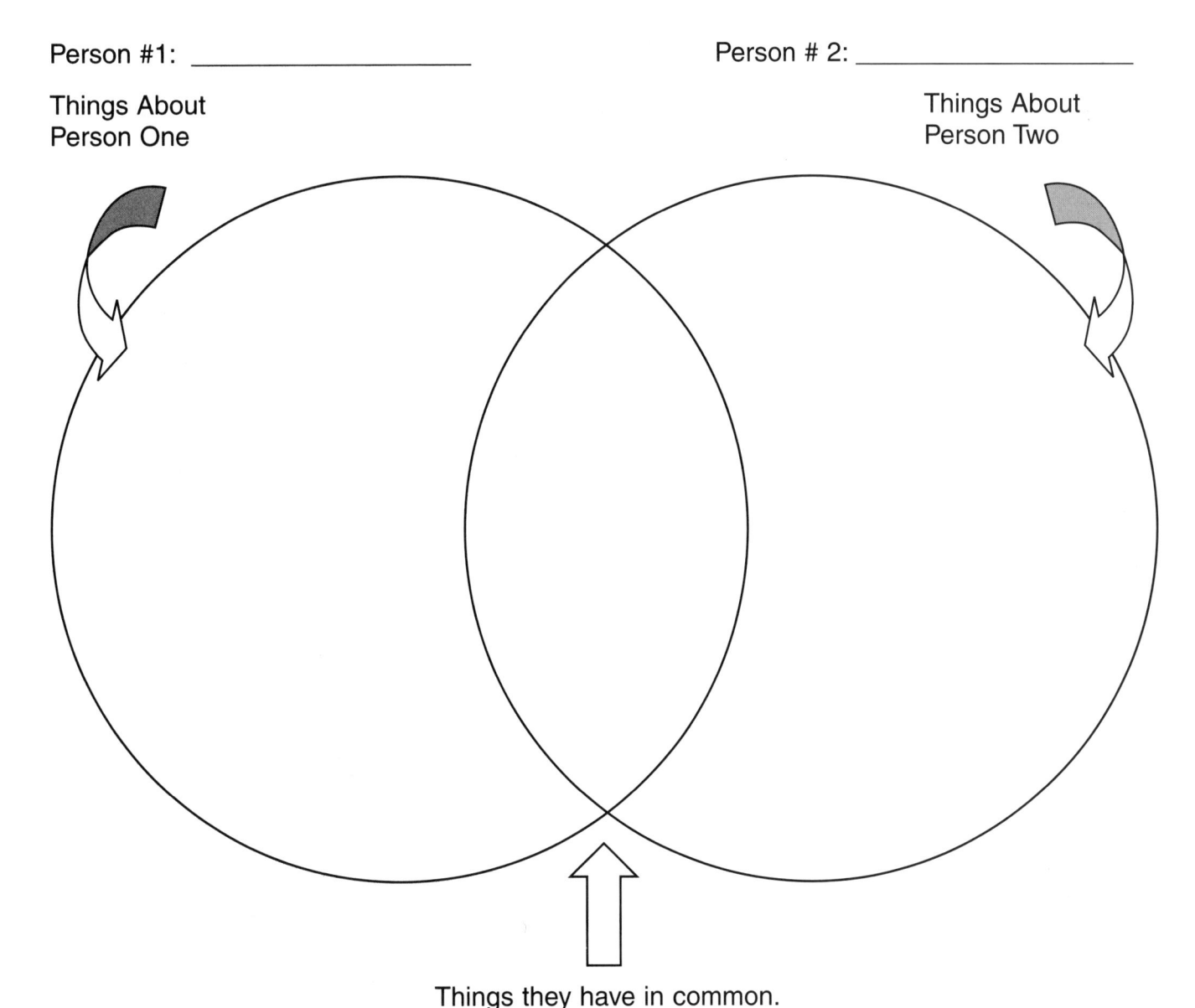

Person #1: _____

Person #2: _____

Things About
Person One

Things About
Person Two

Things they have in common.

©Teacher Created Resources, Inc.   53   #2159 Web Hunts and Virtual Field Trips

Hunting for Social Studies: People of Eminence

Famous or Great?

http://www.teachercreated.com/books/2159   Click on page 52, sites 1-6

Is there a difference between being "famous" and being "great"? Certainly Adolf Hitler is famous because his name and face are well known, but to say that a mass murderer is "great" is a far cry from reality. It seems that there is a difference between being famous and being great, but the difference is hard to find sometimes. In this activity, we'd like you to decide what the difference is between famous and great by studying people of our past and people of today. Perhaps they know the answer to our question!

Key Question: Is there a difference between being "famous" and being "great"?

Directions: Spend some time getting to know the people on the Wall of Inspiration and the companion Web sites. As you read, take notes on some of the people who interest you most. Once you've taken all your notes, leave the computer and complete the rest of this activity sheet either on your own or with a partner or two.

Famous	**Great**
_____ is famous because _____ .	_____ is great because _____ .
_____ is famous because _____ .	_____ is great because _____ .
_____ is famous because _____ .	_____ is great because _____ .
_____ is famous because _____ .	_____ is great because _____ .
_____ is famous because _____ .	_____ is great because _____ .
You can call people famous when…	You can call people great when…

1. Can someone who is great be famous? _____ Example: _____
2. Can someone who is famous be great? _____ Example: _____
3. Can someone be great but not famous? _____ Example: _____
4. Can someone be famous but not great? _____ Example: _____
5. What is the difference between famous and great? _____
6. Which would you rather be? _____

Hunting for Social Studies: People of Eminence

From Here to There

http://www.teachercreated.com/books/2159   Click on page 52, sites 1-6

One of the great things about studying people of eminence is that we have the opportunity to admire people for their contributions, their abilities, and their attitudes. Sometimes, when we come across persons of strength, conviction, or character, we can even aspire to be more like them. In this activity you'll get to make a Path of Life which will bring you closer to having some of those skills and qualities you admire in the people you've chosen to study.

Key Question: What would I have to do in order to become more like one of these people I admire?

Directions: Use the Wall of Inspiration and the companion Web sites listed above to read and learn more about some of the people of eminence in our world and in our past. Choose one person whom you would most like to be like when you grow up. Choose carefully and wisely and then make a Path of Life which will bring you closer to your goal of living a life that reflects your wish to be more like the person you selected. Fill in the goal boxes with mini-goals which will help you meet your main goal.

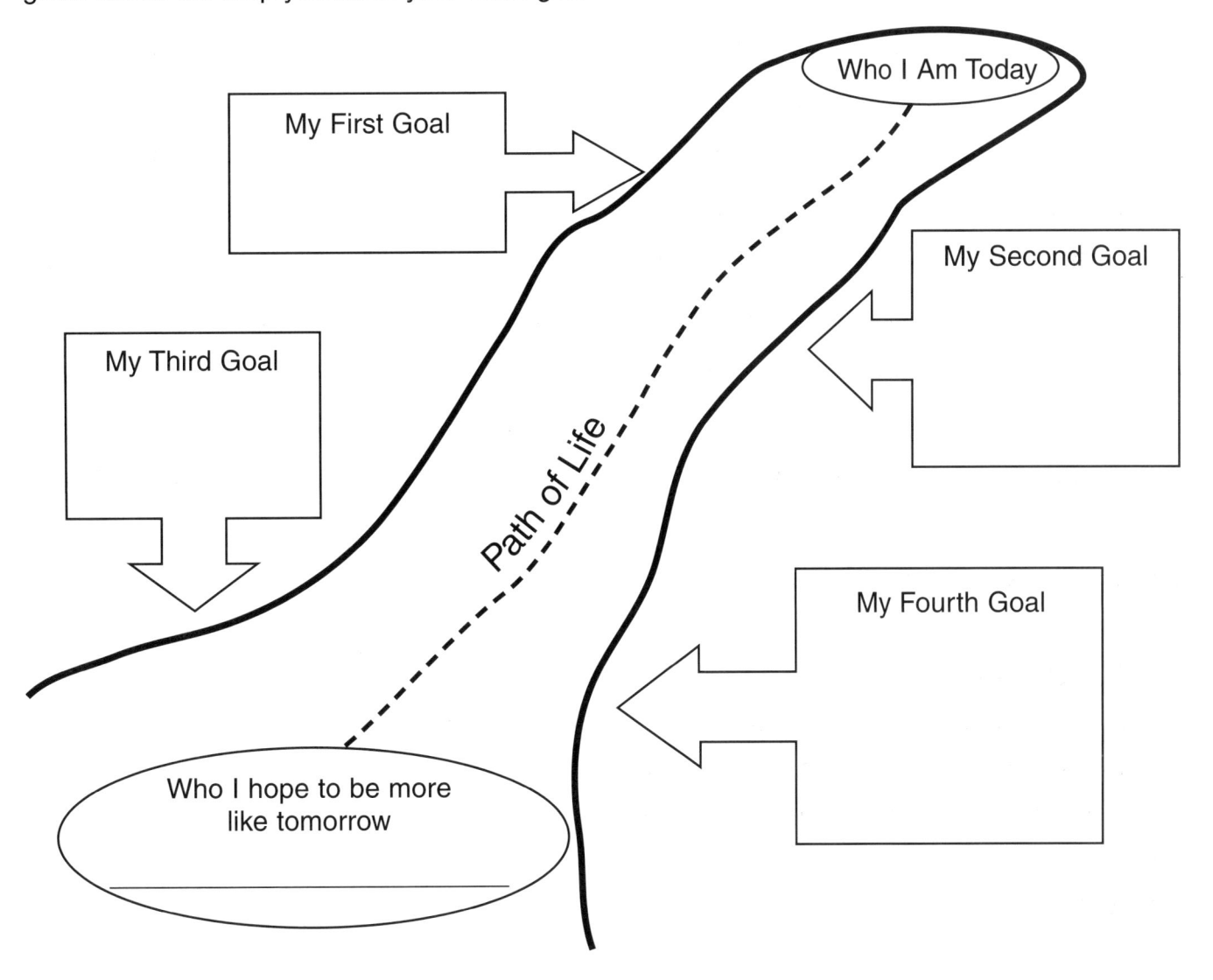

- Who I Am Today
- My First Goal
- My Second Goal
- My Third Goal
- Path of Life
- My Fourth Goal
- Who I hope to be more like tomorrow

©Teacher Created Resources, Inc.   55   #2159 Web Hunts and Virtual Field Trips

Hunting for Social Studies: U.S. History

Building a New Nation

Background

The Revolutionary War period is one of the most vibrant and exciting times in U.S. history. On the backs of the brave words that were spoken and written during these trying times a nation was built. During this hunt your students will gain a deeper understanding for the events that created our nation. It is recommended that these activities follow rather than precipitate a teaching unit on the Revolution.

Objectives

The student will construct a time line of the Revolutionary War.

The student will evaluate and assess events from this time period in order to ascertain their importance/priority.

The student will write a first-person account of a singular event from this period.

The student will construct an interactive experience designed to help his/her peers learn the facts of the Revolutionary War.

The Hunt

Activity One: Timeliners, Inc.

Key Question: How can the Revolutionary War be best represented on a time line?

Preparation: Prepare a list of ten events, names, and places significant to the American Revolution.

Activity Two: Journal It!

Key Question: What would it have been like to have been alive during the Revolutionary War?

Activity Three: ACME Game Makers

Focus Point: Create a board game based on the events, places, and people of the Revolutionary War.

Focus Web Site

Three Cheers for the Red, White, and Blue

Go to *http://www.teachercreated.com/books/2159*

Click on page 56, site 1

Companion Sites

Go to *http://www.teachercreated.com/books/2159*

Schoolhouse Rock	Click on page 56, site 2
The History Place: American Revolution	Click on page 56, site 3
Jump Back in Time: American Revolution	Click on page 56, site 4
The Road to Revolution	Click on page 56, site 5

Hunting for Social Studies: U.S. History

Timeliners, Inc.

http://www.teachercreated.com/books/2159   Click on page 56, sites 1-5

Key Question: How can the Revolutionary War be best represented on a time line?

Directions: Your teacher has given you a list of ten items (events, names, and places) which are significant to the American Revolution. Without using a book or notes, complete the time line below. Once you've completed your time line, go to the Web sites listed above to see how your time line compares to theirs! Use the ovals to indicate a few key dates which will put your time line in perspective and use the boxes for the list your teacher gave you.

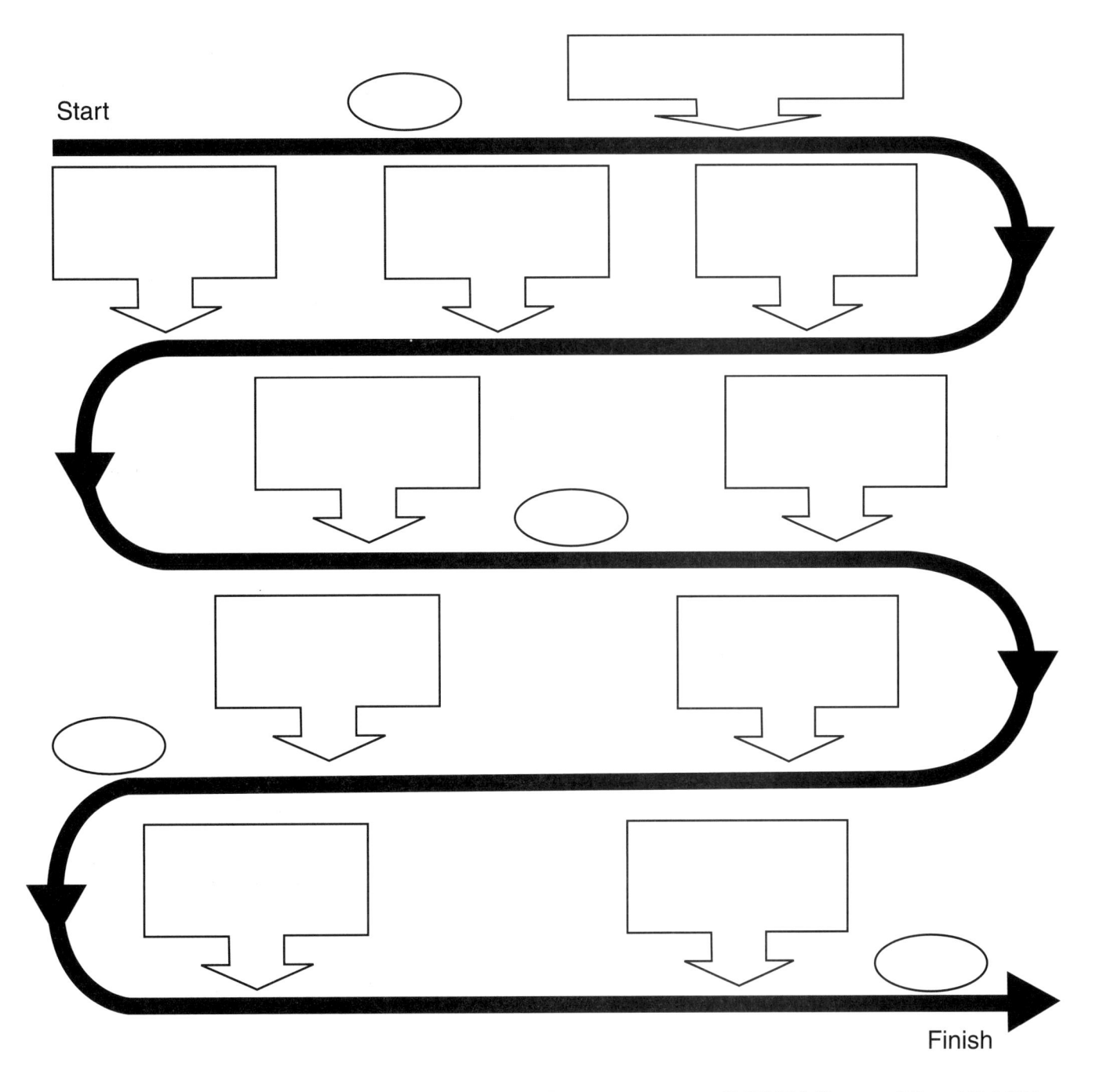

Start

Finish

©Teacher Created Resources, Inc.   57   #2159 *Web Hunts and Virtual Field Trips*

Hunting for Social Studies: U.S. History

Journal It!

http://www.teachercreated.com/books/2159   Click on page 56, sites 1-5

Key Question: What would it have been like to have been alive during the Revolutionary War?

Directions: Select either one important event or influential person from the Revolutionary War period. Use the Web sites listed above to explore your chosen topic. After researching, write a first-person journal entry below. Use as many details as possible to demonstrate your knowledge about the event or the person. When you are done, use a highlighter or crayon to mark every supporting detail in your entry. Count up the highlighted words and give yourself a point for every detail!

Hunting for Social Studies: U.S. History

ACME Game Makers

http://www.teachercreated.com/books/2159   Click on page 56, sites 1-5

Focus Point: Create a board game based on the events, places, and people of the Revolutionary War.

Directions: First, think of one of your favorite board games. Then, use the Web sites above to study the events of the Revolutionary War. Use this activity sheet to help plan your game. Remember that the purpose of this game is to educate players about this period in history while entertaining them. Consider the elements of the game. Will you have Chance/Risk cards (ran out of ammunition, go back three spaces)? Will your board represent New England? Will your game pieces allow for a Colonists' side and a British side? The possibilities are endless. After working through your plan on this sheet, go and build your game!

Thoughts about the game board	Sketch

Thoughts about the steps or "flow" of the game	Cool ideas for pieces, players, strategies, and movements

Hunting for Social Studies: The 50 States

50 States

Background

In this hunt your students will explore, collect, and organize information on the fifty states. In "Only the Best" your students will have the chance to choose one state over all the others according to a ranked criteria which they create themselves. In "Stately Commercials" your students will create an ad campaign to promote moving of the nation's capital to a new state.

Objectives

The student will create a method and criteria for evaluation of the 50 states.

The student will collect and organize information from an online resource.

The student will make and defend a decision based on criteria.

The student will rehearse and apply information based on the 50 states.

The student will participate in the creation of a product designed to persuade.

The student will participate in public speaking.

The Hunt

Activity One: Only the Best
  Key Question: How can I decide which state is "the best"?

Activity Two: Stately Commercials
  Focus Point: Create a commercial promoting one state over the others.

Focus Web Site

Stately Knowledge

  Go to *http://www.teachercreated.com/books/2159*

  Click on page 60, site 1

Companion Sites

  Go to *http://www.teachercreated.com/books/2159*

The U.S. 50	Click on page 60, site 2
Explore the States	Click on page 60, site 3

Hunting for Social Studies: The 50 States

Only the Best

http://www.teachercreated.com/books/2159   Click on page 60, sites 1-3

Key Question: How can I decide which state is "the best"?

Directions: Using the Stately Knowledge and companion Web sites above, choose five states which you would like to "rank" from greatest to least great. Use the chart below to help you organize your information. You'll need to ask yourself one question before you begin: "What makes a state great?" Come up with five answers to that question. For example, you might say that a great sports team, good fishing, lots of museums, closeness to a beach, and a large population make a state great in your opinion. Take your five items (called "Criteria") and put them in the chart below. Then rank each state from 1-5 for each criterium and give it a total score!

What makes a state great?   (1) _____, (2)_____,
(3) _____, (4)_____, (5)_____

Decision-Making Chart	Five Criteria					TOTAL
The States	(1)	(2)	(3)	(4)	(5)	

According to your criteria, which state is the greatest? _____

Hunting for Social Studies: The 50 States

Stately Commercials

http://www.teachercreated.com/books/2159   Click on page 60, sites 1–3

Focus Point: Create a commercial promoting one state over the others.

Directions: The U.S. Government has decided to move the nation's capital to a new location. Your job as the Creative Director of ACME Advertising Agency is to convince the president to choose your favorite state to serve as the new national capital. Use the advertising planning sheet below to guide you in creating your advertising campaign. Your campaign may be radio, television, print, or anything else. It's all up to you! No matter what kind of campaign you run, make sure to make all your planning decisions before you get started! Feel free to work with a creative team to design your campaign. Use the Web sites above to complete your research about the state you choose.

Advertising Planning Sheet

Focal Point: What state am I going to promote in my campaign? _____		
The great things about this state	The OK things about this state	The not-so-great things about this state

The kind of campaign product I'm going to create (circle two):

    Print Ad.   TV Commercial   Radio Commercial

    Internet Ad.   Billboard   Door To Door

Checklist of things to do:

_____ Make a catchy jingle about the state

_____ Get a big-name star to appear in commercials and ads

_____ Design the layout of print ads, Internet ads, or billboards

_____ Design storyboards for radio/TV commercials

_____ Write a script for TV and radio ads

Make sure that you highlight the great things about your state and downplay the not-so-great things! Also, make sure that your products answer the question, "Why would this state be the best place to put the capital?"

Hunting for Social Studies: Maps

Map Attack!

Background

Maps are such an important part of our lives. From weather forecasting to political functions, maps help us to understand the world around us better. In this hunt your students will be asked to review information on a variety of map styles and answer questions to go along with the information. Additionally, your learners will be asked to make a map of their own faces in order to appreciate the challenge that is mapmaking!

Objectives

The student will read nonfiction text on a Web site.

The student will answer comprehension questions based on online reading.

The student will create a grid map of a familiar territory.

The Hunt

Activity One: All About Maps

Key Question: How many kinds of maps are there and what are they used for?

Teacher Note: Consider using this activity in two ways – either as a learning and discovery tool (take the activity sheet to the computer for data collection) or as an assessment tool (use the activity sheet to check retention after the students have left the Web site).

Activity Two: Face Off!

Focus Point: Mapmaking practice can be fun.

Materials: mirrors (big enough to see whole face at once)

Teacher Note: In order to help students to see the difference between making a grid map with an aerial view and a partial view, you might want to ask some students to use a small mirror (where they can't see their entire faces at one time). Also, consider asking your students to add color codes to indicate the elevations of their faces. They could easily turn those into relief maps of their own faces!

Focus Web Site

Maps & Globes

Go to *http://www.teachercreated.com/books/2159*

Click on page 63, site 1

Companion Sites

Go to *http://www.teachercreated.com/books/2159*

Color Landforms of the U.S.	Click on page 63, site 2
U.S. Map	Click on page 63, site 3

©Teacher Created Resources, Inc.

Hunting for Social Studies: Maps

All About Maps

http://www.teachercreated.com/books/2159   Click on page 63, site 1

Key Question: How many kinds of maps are there, and what are they used for?

Directions: Use the Map Web site to answer the following questions about maps.

1. How many different kinds of maps are there? _____

    Name them: _____

2. Name one thing that every map uses: _____

3. Which map is the newest kind of map? _____ Why is it new? _____

    _____

4. Why do maps have scales? _____

5. What kind of map shows the boundaries of countries, regions, states, etc.? _____

6. Why is it important to have maps that show boundaries? What would happen if we didn't have these kinds of maps? _____

    _____

    _____

7. Name three things that a weather map will usually show: _____

    _____

8. How are grids helpful when working with maps? _____

    _____

9. How can historical maps help us to understand our history better? _____

    _____

10. What is a globe? _____

11. What is latitude? _____

12. What is longitude? _____

13. How do latitude and longitude help us? _____

14. Without latitude and longitude how would life be different? _____

    _____

Hunting for Social Studies: Maps

Face Off!

http://www.teachercreated.com/books/2159   Click on page 63, site 1

Focus Point: Mapmaking practice can be fun.

Directions: Use the Maps Web site to review the information on using grids when working with maps. Once you've reviewed that information, you can make a map of a place you know very well: your face! Use the mirror your teacher supplied to draw a picture of your face. Once you're done, answer the questions below!

	A	B	C	D	E
1					
2					
3					
4					
5					

1. What is in B-3? _____ D-4? _____

2. My nose is mostly in grid _____ .

3. My mouth takes up _____ grid boxes. It is in these grid boxes: _____

4. One eye is in grid _____, and one eye is in grid _____ .

Hunting for the Environment: Take Action

Take Action!

Background

The environment is a great concern for all of us. In this hunt your students will be learning about ways they can help to save the environment, encouraging others to lend a hand, and discovering ways your city can make changes. The main site for this hunt is a kid-friendly, information-rich site which has a mountain of information on it. Because of the wealth of information, it's ideal for information management practice.

Objectives

- The student will explore an information-rich Web environment in order to collect data.
- The student will identify and categorize steps he/she can take to make a difference in the environment.
- The student will use a letter writing campaign to encourage others to use specific Earth-saving strategies.
- The student will participate in an online simulation.
- The student will recognize the cause and effect relationships between human interventions and the environment.

The Hunt

Activity One: I Can Make a Difference
   Key Question: What can I do to help save the environment?

Activity Two: Letter Writing
   Key Question: How can I influence other people to do more to save the environment?

Activity Three: Lessons from "Dumptown"
   Key Question: How can cities influence their environment?

Focus Web Site

Recycle City

   Go to *http://www.teachercreated.com/books/2159*

   Click on page 66, site 1

Companion Sites

   Go to *http://www.teachercreated.com/books/2159*

E-Patrol	Click on page 66, site 2
On the Trail of the Missing Ozone	Click on page 66, site 3
How Can Kids Help?	Click on page 66, site 4

Hunting for the Environment: Take Action

I Can Make a Difference

http://www.teachercreated.com/books/2159   Click on page 66, site 1

Key Question: What can I do to help save the environment?

Directions: Spend time exploring the Recycle City Web site. Really get into all the nooks and crevices so that you can learn all there is to know about protecting the environment. Make sure you take your "I Can Make A Difference Plan" with you to the Web site so that as you read you can record nine things you can do to make a difference. Once you've visited all the places in Recycle City, review your plan and add dates to the "Do By" column. Keep your plan handy so that you can record what happened to your good intentions. We started you out with one example – now it's your turn!

I Can Make A Difference Plan		
I'm going to…	**Do By**	**I Did It!**
Buy recycled pencils	next Tuesday	On Monday I bought my supplies for class, and I bought recycled pencils (and notebooks too)!

Hunting for the Environment: Take Action

Letter Writing

http://www.teachercreated.com/books/2159   Click on page 66, site 1

Key Question: How can I influence other people to do more to save the environment?

Directions: In our last activity you focused on ways you could save the world; now it's time to spread the word to others. Use the Recycle City Web site to get a few ideas of things businesses, schools, or other adults might be able to do a pitch in to help save the environment. Once you've found a suggestion you'd like to share with someone else, use this activity page to help deliver your message!

Date: _____

Dear _____ ,

My name is _____ . In school recently I've been studying ways to protect the environment. We've been using a really great Web site called Recycle City (*http://www.epa.gov/recyclecity/*) to help us learn.

While I was learning more about recycling, I found a way that you might be able to help the environment, too. I think you might be able to help the environment by using this strategy I found:

_____.

I'd like to encourage you to use this strategy for two weeks so that you can see what kind of a difference it makes in the environment! I know that you'll want to participate in helping to save the planet.

Thank you so much for your time.

Sincerely,

_____

Student in _____ School

PS: Feel free to write to us and let us know how things turned out!

Hunting for the Environment: Take Action

Lessons from "Dumptown"

http://www.teachercreated.com/books/2159   Click on page 66, site 1

Key Question: How can cities influence their environment?

Directions: Play the Dumptown game on the Recycle City Web site. It might be a good idea to play with a partner so that you can take turns keeping track of the changes you've made in Dumptown. Use the cause and effect chart below to show the changes that you made (causes) and the effects your changes had on the town.

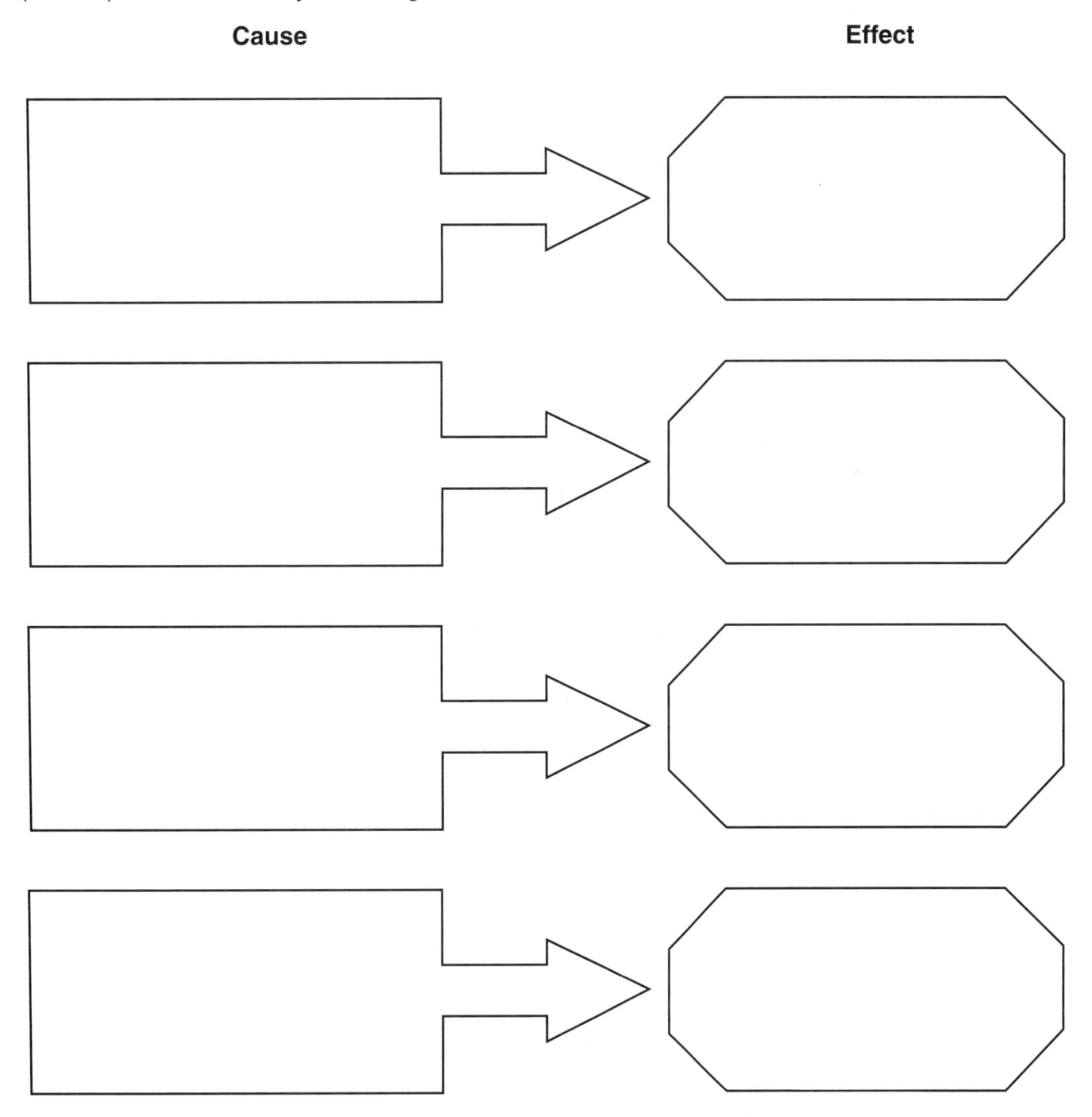

Cause	Effect
→	
→	
→	
→	

Hunting for the Environment: Endangered Animals

Threatened, Endangered, Extinct, Oh My!

Background

The incredible numbers of threatened, endangered, and extinct animals are overwhelming. They serve as a message that we must make changes in the way we affect the world around us. In this hunt your students will have the opportunity to sort through kid-friendly information about endangered animals in the hopes of learning more about the causes and effects of endangered animals.

Objectives

The student will collect and organize information from nonfiction Web resources.

The student will summarize nonfiction text into smaller chunks.

The student will evaluate text to find relevant information.

The student will recognize the causes of extinction.

The student will recognize that there are often underlying causes beneath main causes of complex problems.

The Hunt

Activity One: Just the Facts, Ma'am.

Key Question: What are the causes of extinction for certain animals?

Activity Two: The Path of Responsibility: Follow the Cause

Key Question: Are there supporting causes which will help us to better understand the threats to our animal populations?

Teacher Note: Try this extension as a class project – take one endangered or threatened animal (preferably one that lives in or near your area) and build a responsibility path like the ones on page 72, but this time challenge yourselves to bring the boxes all the way back to you (the students and yourself). Don't forget that inaction is as dangerous as action sometimes!

Focus Web Site

Animal List

Go to *http://www.teachercreated.com/books/2159*

Click on page 70, site 1

Companion Sites

Go to *http://www.teachercreated.com/books/2159*

Endangered Species Profiles	Click on page 70, site 2
Protecting Endangered Species from Pesticides	Click on page 70, site 3
WWF Fact Sheets	Click on page 70, site 4
Endangered Animals Student Story Project	Click on page 70, site 5

Hunting for the Environment: Endangered Animals

Just the Facts, Ma'am

http://www.teachercreated.com/books/2159   Click on page 70, site 1

Key Question: What are the causes of extinction for certain animals?

Directions: Use the Animal List Web site to learn more about some of the world's most popular threatened and endangered animals. Practice your recordkeeping and information management skills by completing the Animals in Danger chart below. Choose six of your favorite animals from the Web site and collect the data needed for the chart.

Animals in Danger

The Animals	The Data		
	Where's home?	Fascinating Fact	What's causing extinction?

Hunting for the Environment: Endangered Animals

The Path of Responsibility: Follow the Cause

http://www.teachercreated.com/books/2159   Click on page 70, site 1

Sometimes there are supporting causes for problems in our world. For example is it the moviemaker's fault that there is too much violence in the movies showing at our local movie theatres? Sure, but only partially. It's also the movegoer's fault for paying money to see movies with too much violence. This example shows a shared responsibility for the problem of movie violence. How about animal extinction? Are there any shared responsibilities there? We think you might be able to find some if you take a close look at the causes of extinction. Remember to ask yourself one simple question: "Why?"

Key Question: Are there supporting causes which will help us to better understand the threats to our animal populations?

Directions: For each animal listed, use the Web sites to find the main causes of endangerment. Then work backwards to discover what (or who!) the supporting causes are. When you discover a cause, just ask yourself "Why is that happening?" and you'll probably find a supporting cause.

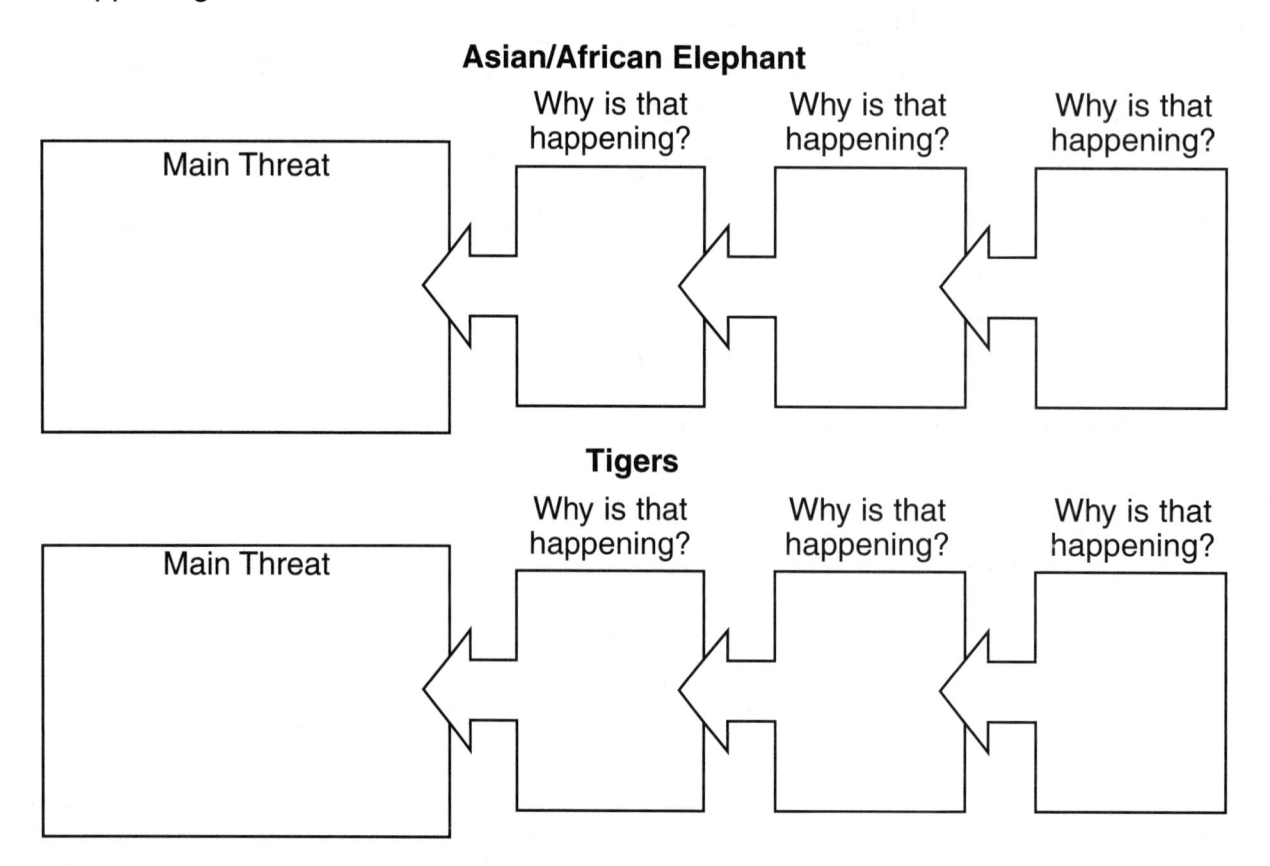

Asian/African Elephant

| Main Threat | Why is that happening? | Why is that happening? | Why is that happening? |

Tigers

| Main Threat | Why is that happening? | Why is that happening? | Why is that happening? |

A final thought: (Use the back of this page to respond to these questions.)

Do you see any patterns in the supporting causes? Any similarities? Anything that makes you curious? Anything that is easily fixed?

Hunting for the Environment: Landforms

Landforms

Background

A major part of understanding our environment is knowing about the land on which we live. Though only ¼ of the Earth is land, there are a variety of forms that land can take. The kinds of landforms we have on this planet greatly affect the lifestyles of its people. In this hunt your students will need to show their understanding of the differences among landform environments by creating a vehicle which will adapt to each environment. Your learners will also get to test their vocal chords when they create songs which share newly-learned landform information.

Objectives

The student will read and interpret information from a nonfiction Web resource.

The student will synthesize information and will create a product to demonstrate his/her understanding of the information.

The student will construct a new framework (musical) for the retelling of old information.

The Hunt

Activity One: Let's Go Four Wheelin'
   Key Question: Can we show what we know about landforms through car creations?

Activity Two: Sing, Sing a Song
   Focus Point: Joining information and music can help me to remember cool stuff!

Focus Web Site

Landforms of the World

   Go to *http://www.teachercreated.com/books/2159*

   Click on page 73, site 1

Companion Site

   Go to *http://www.teachercreated.com/books/2159*

Landforms   Click on page 73, site 2

Hunting for the Environment: Landforms

Let's Go Four Wheelin'

http://www.teachercreated.com/books/2159   Click on page 73, site 1

Key Question: Can we show what we know about landforms through car creations?

Directions: Use the Landforms Web site to learn all you can about different kinds of landforms. We recommend you go online with a partner and that you take a notepad with you so that you can take great notes! Once you've learned all there is to know about each kind of landform environment, your job is to create a car that can manage each kind of landform. Would a "mountain car" look much different from an "island car"? What would be different about it? What special details and options would a "volcano car" need to have? Your car designs need to show that you really understand the kind of terrain and special circumstances of each of the landforms listed below. Be creative and zany! Remember to buckle up and turn on the tunes!

Landforms	Car Names	Sketches (Use arrows to label special features.)
Volcanoes		
Mountains		
Islands		
Plateaus		

Which one would you most like to have? Why? _____

Hunting for the Environment: Landforms

Sing, Sing a Song

http://www.teachercreated.com/books/2159   Click on page 73, site 1

Focus Point: Joining information and music can help me to remember cool stuff!

Directions: Use the Landforms Web site to learn all about the different kinds of landforms. As you read the information on the site, take sparse notes (just the highlights) on the chart below so that you'll have the information you need to create a landforms sing-along! You might want to use a tune from a song or a jingle that you know already. Once you have your notes and you've decided on a tune, it's time to build your song. Try using the sections of the chart below to break your information into the stanzas of a song! When you're all ready, belt out a cool landforms tune!

	Note Takin' Side	Song Makin' Side
Islands		
Mountains		
Volcanoes		
Continents		

Introduction to Virtual Field Trips

Pack your bags and climb aboard! We're off to discover new places and fun-filled locations!

On the following pages you will find field trips that span a variety of topics from trips to the ocean to trips to the past. Each trip has a key question or focus point which helps your students stay focused on their topic.

Key Questions and Statements

Trips of Culture

Does it help to think about a place before going there?

Can knowing one measurement of one part of an object lead you to figuring out its other measurements?

What do our country's national symbols represent?

What can we learn about an artist by looking at his inspiration and his work?

Is it possible to translate a work of art into a work of words?

Can baseball cards help us learn to write better?

How can you tell which photograph is best?

Trips to the Water

How much do I really know about oceans?

What do oceans do for us, and what can we do for oceans?

How many different ways can you teach someone something new?

Where are coral reefs located, and which ones are in danger?

What can students do to help protect the coral reefs?

What is the story of man's effect on the Everglades?

What animals live in the Everglades?

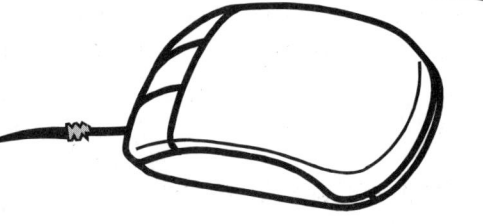

Key Questions and Statements (cont.)

Trips in Time

What was life like in ancient Egypt?

How did ancient Egypt communicate?

How were the pyramids built?

What are the important facts represented by the Freedom Trail?

Can we turn the Freedom Trail into a giant web?

Who was Leonardo da Vinci, and what did he do?

What would my life have been like as a child during the Renaissance?

Trips in Space

What makes me curious about outer space?

Use the Internet for solar system research.

What would aliens from different planets in our solar system look like?

What were the major events on the trip to the moon and back?

How can photographs be used to tell a story?

What kind of module would you add to the space stations if you could?

What would it be like to live in outer space?

Trips to Nature

What lives inside the rain forest?

What are the main threats to the health of the rain forest?

What lives in each level of the rain forest, and is it similar to my habitat?

What might the first person to discover the Galapagos Islands have written in his diary?

Can we pass our knowledge on to others through games?

What do we think of when we think of the desert?

Are desert animals special?

Trips to Famous Places

What is Stonehenge?

How was Stonehenge built?

Why were Washington, Lincoln, Roosevelt, and Jefferson chosen to be the faces of Mount Rushmore?

Which of today's personalities or leaders would be picked for a current Mt. Rushmore?

Do Americans use many walls? What for and why?

Trips of Culture: The Statue of Liberty

America, The Beautiful

Background

Part of the spirit that is our American culture is the pride we feel when we see our flag flapping in a summer breeze, when we see bursts of fireworks in the July sky, or when we hear our national anthem. These symbols are part of the fabric of life in America. Perhaps one of the best-known symbols is the Statue of Liberty – that green-tinted goddess of freedom and protection. Let's take a trip and visit her.

Objectives

The student will take time to think about a place before visiting it.

The student will use pre-instruction data to evaluate progress.

The student will produce a grid drawing of an object.

The student will use a known measurement to estimate unknown measurements.

The student will collect and organize specific data from an online resource.

The student will interpret and synthesize data into a key phrase.

The Trip

Activity One: Pre-Trip Quiz!
Key Question: Does it help to think about a place before going there?

Activity Two: How Tall is a Legend?
Key Question: Can knowing one measurement of one part of an object lead you to figuring out its other measurements?

Activity Three: The Symbols of a Nation
Key Question: What do our country's national symbols represent?

Focus Web Site

The Statue of Liberty

Go to *http://www.teachercreated.com/books/2159*
Click on page 78, site 1

Companion Sites

Go to *http://www.teachercreated.com/books/2159*

The Statue of Liberty: Student Project	Click on page 78, site 2
The Statue of Liberty: Live Cam	Click on page 78, site 3
Francis Scott Key	Click on page 78, site 4
The American Bald Eagle	Click on page 78, site 5
I Am the Flag	Click on page 78, site 6
The Liberty Bell Museum	Click on page 78, site 7
The Liberty Bell	Click on page 78, site 8

Trips of Culture: The Statue of Liberty

Name: _____ Date: _____

Pre-Trip Quiz!

Key Question: Does it help to think about a place before going there?

Directions: Before our class trip to see the Statue of Liberty, it might be fun to do some pre-trip thinking. Answer these questions now, and we'll check on them after our trip to see how close we came to the real thing!

1. When was the Statue of Liberty built? _____
2. What time of day can we go and what time do we have to leave? _____
3. How much will it cost you to go see Liberty? _____
4. How do you get to the statue? _____
5. How many lines will you have to stand in? _____
6. How many torches are there on Liberty Island? _____
7. How high can you go inside Liberty? _____
8. What city can you see from the top of Liberty? _____
9. What color did Liberty's face used to be? _____
10. What famous words are written on Liberty's pedestal? _____
_____
_____
11. How long will the trip to see Liberty take you? _____
12. Draw a picture of Liberty's face:

Keep this paper until after your trip so that you can see how close you came to the correct answers for these questions!

©Teacher Created Resources, Inc.   79   #2159 Web Hunts and Virtual Field Trips

Trips of Culture: The Statue of Liberty

How Tall is a Legend?

http://www.teachercreated.com/books/2159   Click on page 78, site 1

Key Question: Can knowing one measurement of one part of an object lead you to figuring out its other measurements?

Directions:

1. Draw a sketch of Lady Liberty in the grid on the left-hand side of this page.

2. Travel through the photo tour of the Statue of Liberty Web site and pay close attention to any mentions of the size of the statue. Take notes in the Data Collection Area below.

3. Use your drawing and the information you gathered from the Web site to label the height and width of the parts of the statue listed on this page. Be sure to show your work!

Data Collection Area

Height of statue: _____

Width of statue: _____

Length of arm: _____

Length of torch: _____

Width of book: _____

Width of head: _____

Trips of Culture: The Statue of Liberty

The Symbols of a Nation

http://www.teachercreated.com/books/2159   Click on page 78, sites 1-8

Key Question: What do our country's national symbols represent?

Directions: Use the Statue of Liberty Web site and the companion sites listed above to learn more about the symbols of our nation. As you travel from symbol to symbol, fill in the chart below. When you're done, create a new national symbol to add to the history books!

The Symbols	What this represents to American citizens:	How long has this been a symbol?
The Statue of Liberty		
The American Flag		
The Bald Eagle		
The Liberty Bell		
My New Symbol		

©Teacher Created Resources, Inc.   81   #2159 Web Hunts and Virtual Field Trips

Trips of Culture: Monet's Garden

Monet's Garden

Background

Certainly, when people think of culture, they think of great works of art by artists such as Monet. In this trip we'll travel to Monet's Garden–the garden of inspiration.

Objectives

The student will explore an interactive Web site.

The student will recognize the relationship between inspiration and creation.

The student will use descriptive words in order to better understand a painting.

The student will write a creative story based on a painting.

The Trip

Activity One: Discovering Monet

Key Question: What can we learn about an artist by looking at his inspiration and his work?

Activity Two: Painting with Words

Key Question: Is it possible to translate a work of art into a work of words?

Focus Web Site

Monet's Garden

Go to *http://www.teachercreated.com/books/2159*

Click on page 82, site 1

Companion Sites

Go to *http://www.teachercreated.com/books/2159*

Monet Gallery	Click on page 82, site 2
Art Kids Rule!	Click on page 82, site 3
Monet Biography	Click on page 82, site 4
Monet's Garden, Giverny	Click on page 82, site 5

Trips of Culture: Monet's Garden

Discovering Monet

http://www.teachercreated.com/books/2159   Click on page 82, site 1

It is a well-known fact that Monet was inspired by the gardens at Giverny. The scenes, colors, and light from the gardens show up again and again in his paintings. With enough study, we can begin to understand a little bit about Claude Monet, the man.

Key Question: What can we learn about an artist by looking at his inspiration and his work?

Directions: Spend some time touring through the flower garden and the water garden on the Monet's Garden Web site. On the top section of this paper, take notes on what you see: colors, objects, shapes, buildings, and especially colors. Keep taking notes througout the tour. Once your visit is over, use the bottom section of the page to draw some conclusions about Monet the man.

The Gardens at Giverny	
The Flower Garden	The Water Garden

Conclusions About Monet

1. I think Monet's favorite colors were _____ and _____ because _____.

2. I think Monet's favorite season was _____ because _____.

3. Monet probably liked to paint in the (*circle one*) morning/afternoon/evening because _____.

4. If Monet had been employed at something other than painting, I think it would have been _____ because _____.

5. Other thoughts I have about Monet…   (Use the back!)

©Teacher Created Resources, Inc.   #2159 Web Hunts and Virtual Field Trips

Trips of Culture: Monet's Garden

Painting with Words

http://www.teachercreated.com/books/2159   Click on page 82, sites 1-2

Many artists say that their paintings tell a story. In this activity you're going to have the chance to translate one of Monet's paintings into a story.

Key Question: Is it possible to translate a work of art into a work of words?

Directions: Use the Monet's Garden and the Monet Gallery Web sites to look at some of Monet's inspirations and his paintings. Once you're familiar with his work, select one painting that you really like. Use the space below to turn the painting into a story. A story starter is already there for you.

Painting Title: _____

Monet

One day I stepped through a magical frame and found myself…

_____
_____
_____
_____
_____
_____
_____
_____
_____
_____
_____
_____
_____

Trips of Culture: Baseball Hall of Fame

Take Me Out to the Ball Game

Background

Baseball is America's sport. It has been part of Americana for generations. It helps us to define our seasons, moods, and dreams. This field trip takes us to Cooperstown—to the Baseball Hall of Fame. Here we will find much to explore, so grab a ball and glove and let's head out to the ballpark.

Objectives

The student will navigate to a specific point on a Web site.

The student will make an evaluative choice based on printed data.

The student will summarize text in order to present information.

The student will evaluate an object according to self-defined criteria.

The student will construct and implement an evaluative tool (chart).

The Trip

Activity One: Trade Ya!
   Key Question: Can baseball cards help us learn to write better?

Activity Two: You Be the Judge
   Key Question: How can you tell which photograph is best?

Focus Web Site

The National Baseball Hall of Fame

   Go to *http://www.teachercreated.com/books/2159*

Click on page 85, site 1

Companion Sites

   Go to *http://www.teachercreated.com/books/2159*

A Short History of the Single-Season Home Run Record	Click on page 85, site 2
1998 Hall of Fame Photo Contest Winners	Click on page 85, site 3
1999 Hall of Fame Photo Contest Winners	Click on page 85, site 4
2000 Hall of Fame Photo Contest Winners	Click on page 85, site 5
2001 Hall of Fame Photo Contest Winners	Click on page 85, site 6

©Teacher Created Resources, Inc.   #2159 Web Hunts and Virtual Field Trips

Trips of Culture: Baseball Hall of Fame

Trade Ya!

http://www.teachercreated.com/books/2159   Click on page 85, site 1

Key Question: Can baseball cards help us learn to write better?

Directions: Go to The National Baseball Hall of Fame Web site and check out the *Online Exhibits* area. There you will find a section entitled *A Short History of the Single-Season Home Run Record*. Read through that section of the Web site. Choose from the players on the left side of the page and learn more about their incredible home run-hitting seasons. This will be the hard part: *choose two players* who you think are the best players out of that group of sluggers. In the spaces below, create two baseball cards, one for each player. You have room to do a front and back for each card. The front side should show a picture of the player. The flip side should give details about his impressive slug-filled season. Use the information from the player's page to write a summary of your player's awesome slugfest!

Player One: _____

Player Two: _____

#2159 Web Hunts and Virtual Field Trips ©Teacher Created Resources, Inc.

Trips of Culture: Baseball Hall of Fame

You Be the Judge

http://www.teachercreated.com/books/2159   Click on page 85, sites 3-6

Key Question: How can you tell which photograph is best?

Directions: Before you begin, you'll need to answer the following question.

What five qualities are most important to me in a sports photograph? (Think of qualities like these: clarity of picture, the subject, the emotions it brings out in me, the composition, the colors, the mood.) List your five choices down the left-hand column of the chart.

Next, use the Hall of Fame Photo Contest winners on the Web sites above to complete the rest of this activity. You'll probably want to choose your four favorite photographs and print them out so that you can take a long hard look at them. Use the chart below to rate your choices on a scale from 1 (lowest) to 10 (highest). Did you agree with their judges?

Photographs

Photo Qualities	Photo #1	Photo #2	Photo #3	Photo #4

Trips to the Water: Oceans

Water, Water Everywhere

Background

The oceans of the world define our planet. Understanding them can help us to understand our home. In this trip we travel to Mother Ocean to learn what we can and question what we think we know.

Objectives

The student will complete a K/W/L chart based on his/her knowledge of oceans.

The student will recognize the reciprocal relationship between humans and their ocean environments.

The student will extend his/her thinking past the presented content into theory.

The student will read, digest, and present new information to a group.

The student will create a variety of products designed to be educational tools.

The student will participate in a group oral presentation.

The Trip

Activity One: What Do I Know? What Do I Want to Know? What Did I Learn?
   Key Question: How much do I really know about oceans?

Activity Two: It's a Two-Way Street
   Key Question: What do oceans do for us, and what can we do for oceans?

Activity Three: It's All Up to You!
   Key Question: How many different ways can you teach someone something new?
   Teacher Note: Divide the students into groups and assign topics from the Web site.

Focus Web Sites

Oceans and Coastal Protection Kids' Page
   Go to *http://www.teachercreated.com/books/2159*
   Click on page 88, site 1

Companion Sites

   Go to *http://www.teachercreated.com/books/2159*

Neptune's Web	Click on page 88, site 2
Cetaceans	Click on page 88, site 3
What's It Like Where You Live?—Temperate Oceans	Click on page 88, site 4
PBS: Secrets of the Ocean Realm	Click on page 88, site 5

Trips to the Water: Oceans

What Do I Know? What Do I Want to Know? What Did I Learn?

http://www.teachercreated.com/books/2159   Click on page 88, sites 1-2

Key Question: How much do I really know about oceans?

Directions: Before you read anything, complete the left side of the K/W/L chart below. The "K" stands for "Know," so write down everything you know about oceans in that column. The "W" stands for "Want to Know," so brainstorm at least five questions you have about oceans. After you've done those two sections, go and visit the ocean – on the Internet, that is! Explore the two focus Web sites for this field trip.

When you're finished reading, take some time to complete the right side. The "L" stands for "Learned." Write down everything you learned from your visit to the ocean. If you have the time you might want to color-code the questions you have in the middle sections and any corresponding answers you found on the right-hand section! If you didn't find your answers, check with some of the other ocean travelers. Maybe they found something you missed!

K	W	L

Trips to the Water: Oceans

It's a Two-Way Street

http://www.teachercreated.com/books/2159   Click on page 88, sites 1-5

The relationship between the ant and the picnic is clear. Without the picnic, the ant has no food and without the ant, the picnic has no scavengers to clean up after it. This kind of relationship, where both parties need each other, is called a symbiotic relationship. Human beings sometimes ignore the symbiotic relationship they have with their planet. Our planet provides us with food to eat and water to drink, and yet we poison the water and destroy the land. In this activity you'll need to come up with some ideas on different ways we can give back to the ocean that gives us so much.

Key Question: What do oceans do for us, and what can we do for oceans?

Directions: Use the Web sites above in order to complete this thoughtful activity. Once you've become familiar with the information available to you about our oceans, answer the questions on each side of this chart. Come up with as many good answers as you possibly can – stretch your thinking and make your brain tired!

What does the ocean give to us?	What should we give to the ocean?

Trips to the Water: Oceans

It's All Up to You!

http://www.teachercreated.com/books/2159   Click on page 88, site 4

In this activity YOU are the teacher! Your mission, should you choose to accept it, is to work in a group to teach the rest of your class something about oceans. Most of the work is already done for you – all the research is right there on the Evergreen Project Web site. All you have to do is harvest it and find a creative way to present it.

Key Question: How many different ways can you teach someone something new?

Directions: Use the What's It Like Where You Live?—Temperate Oceans Web site to help you with this activity. Once you get to the site, click on your group topic on the left side of the screen. Read the information carefully. You might want to take notes. (Hint: If you have your teacher's permission, you might even want to print the page!) Once you've gathered all your information, choose three of the activities on the menu below. You'll need to use these products to present this information to the class so that they can understand it - so have fun with it, but stay true to your data! Remember, when you're working with a group, it's always a good idea to divide up the chores! Once you finish your presentation to the class, meet again as a group and take a few notes on how your group did.

Product Menu
(*choose 3*)

_____ Make a poster

_____ Write & sing a song

_____ Build a model

_____ Perform a dance

_____ Write a report

_____ Create a commercial

_____ Do a skit

_____ Conduct an interview

Group Assignments

Name: _____
Job: _____

Name: _____
Job: _____

Name: _____
Job: _____

Name: _____
Job: _____

Name: _____
Job: _____

Name: _____
Job: _____

How'd we do?

Trips to the Water: Coral Reefs

Reef Attack

Background

The coral reefs of this world are some of the most beautiful sights to behold. The sad truth that they are in such danger should bring us to immediate action. In this Trip to the Water, your students will visit the coral reefs in hopes of finding ways to protect them.

Objectives

The student will locate the coral reefs of the world.

The student will read, collect, and organize information from an online resource.

The student will summarize and restate nonfiction text in a meaningful way.

The student will work with a partner to create a product.

The student will analyze nonfiction text in order to extrapolate answers.

The student will compare estimated answers with actual answers.

The Trip

Activity One: Locating Reefs in Trouble
  Key Question: Where are coral reefs located, and which ones are in danger?
Activity Two: So, What Can I Do?
  Key Question: What can students do to help protect the coral reefs?

Focus Web Site

Clickable Map of Coral Reefs

   Go to *http://www.teachercreated.com/books/2159*

   Click on page 92, site 1

Companion Sites

   Go to *http://www.teachercreated.com/books/2159*

Things You Can Do to Help the Coral Reef	Click on page 92, site 2
What is a Coral Reef?	Click on page 92, site 3
What's It Like Where You Live?—Tropical Oceans	Click on page 92, site 4

Trips to the Water: Coral Reefs

Locating Reefs in Trouble

http://www.teachercreated.com/books/2159   Click on page 92, site 1

Key Question: Where are coral reefs located, and which ones are in danger?

Directions: Use the Coral Reefs Web site to complete this activity. Check out the coral reef map and take note of how few coral reefs there are in the world. Now click on the "hot spots," those areas where the coral reefs are in danger. As you click through the map, use this sheet to take notes on the dangers to the coral reef. When you're through, use this information to draft a letter of concern to the people, businesses, or government of that area. Explain to them what you think should be done to protect their precious coral reefs.

Location	What's the Danger?	Who is Responsible?

Trips to the Water: Coral Reefs

So, What Can I Do?

http://www.teachercreated.com/books/2159   Click on page 92, sites 2-4

Key Question: What can students do to help protect the coral reefs?

Directions: Use the Web sites listed above to learn more about the coral reefs – what they are, how they "work," what they do, how they're in danger. After you're done, get together with a partner and discuss an answer to this question: "What can I do to help save the coral reefs?" Brainstorm a list of ideas on the left side of this page. After your conversation is over, go to the Things You Can Do to Help the Coral Reef Web site. While you're there, take notes on the right side of this page. Before calling it quits, color code any matches you found on your right and left sides!

Ideas we thought of	Suggestions from the Web site
How many did you think of? _____	How many did you find? _____

Trips to the Water: The Everglades

River of Grass

Background

The Everglades is one of the most unique environments in the world. In this trip your students will learn more about the history of the Everglades as well as how man has marked that history. They'll also have the chance to create some kid-friendly ways to teach others about the important inhabitants of the Everglades.

Objectives

The student will create a tall tale to explain the history of man's intrusion on the Everglades.

The student will read and interpret nonfiction text in order to create something new.

The student will complete a writer's planning sheet before writing.

The student will read and synthesize nonfiction text from an online source.

The student will create a product, using both artistic and writing skills.

The student will summarize nonfiction text in his/her own words.

The Trip

Activity One: Once Upon a Time
Key Question: What is the story of man's effect on the Everglades?

Activity Two: Whose Home Is This Anyway?
Key Question: What animals live in the Everglades?

Focus Web Site

Everglades National Park (ENP): Past & Present

Go to *http://www.teachercreated.com/books/2159*

Click on page 95, site 1

Companion Sites

Go to *http://www.teachercreated.com/books/2159*

ENP: What Happened?	Click on page 95, site 2
ENP: Endangered Species	Click on page 95, site 3
ENP: Animal Profiles	Click on page 95, site 4
ENP: Species Checklist	Click on page 95, site 5
ENP: Habitats	Click on page 95, site 6
ENP: How Can I Help?	Click on page 95, site 7

Trips to the Water: The Everglades

Once Upon a Time

http://www.teachercreated.com/books/2159   Click on page 95, sites 1-2

Some people say that Paul Bunyon and Babe the Blue Ox actually existed. Others swear that they've seen Bigfoot out in the deep forest. Whether the stories are true or not really isn't important. What is important is that these tall tales help us to pass information from one generation to the next. In this activity you're going to create a tall tale that will tell the story of the Everglades.

Key Question: What is the story of man's effect on the Everglades?

Directions: Read the history of the Everglades on the Web sites above. Once you're familiar with the story of the Everglades, turn it into a Tall Tale. Try to spin your story so that you show one "bad guy" who represents what man has done to the Everglades and one "good guy" (maybe a kid like you?) who convinces everyone to help save the Everglades. Remember that Tall Tales usually have some pretty interesting exaggerations! Write your story on your own paper after using this page to help you plan your work!

The Title: _____

The name of the "bad guy": _____

Description of the "bad guy": _____

_____

Something that's larger than life about this character: _____

_____

The name of the "good guy": _____

Description of the "good guy": _____

_____

Something that's larger than life about this character: _____

_____

Use these boxes to arrange your plot (the events in your story leading to healing the Everglades):

Trips to the Water: The Everglades

Whose Home Is This Anyway?

http://www.teachercreated.com/books/2159   Click on page 95, sites 3-5

Trading cards have made athletes and cartoons famous; maybe they can do the same for the animals of the Everglades!

Key Question: What animals live in the Everglades?

Directions: Read all about the animals of the Everglades on the ENP: Endangered Species and the ENP: Species Checklist Web sites. In the spaces below, create two trading cards for the two Everglades animals your teacher assigned to you. The front of each card should be a color picture of the animal in its habitat. The back of the card should give any information you think would be interesting to someone trading that card. You can use this opportunity to teach the trading card owners a little bit about how to protect these beautiful creatures.

Animal Name: _____

Animal Name: _____

©Teacher Created Resources, Inc.   #2159 Web Hunts and Virtual Field Trips

Trips in Time: Ancient Egypt

Once Upon a Time—A Verrrrry Long Time Ago

Background

Ancient Egypt was a rich culture that still interests us today. From pyramids to mummies to the ancient gods, there is much to be learned from the Egyptians. In this trip we will travel back in time to the days of ancient Egypt. We will pretend to be queens and servants. We will use the language of the pharaohs and solve the mystery of the pyramids. Now let's travel back in time!

Objectives

The student will read and interpret nonfiction text from an online source.

The student will summarize nonfiction text in order to create a product.

The student will work in a team to write and produce a one-act play.

The student will participate in a creative writing activity using an ancient language.

The student will develop a theory based on current knowledge.

The student will analyze expert theories in relationship to his/her own.

The Trip

Activity One: Tell It Like It Was

Key Question: What was life like in ancient Egypt?

Activity Two: Picture Words

Key Question: How did ancient Egyptians communicate?

Teacher Note: You may want to provide some sample ads from a current newspaper to show your students how different ad writing is from regular writing. Using crumpled and torn brown paper bags to write on is a great way to make the writing look old. Also, colored pencils or thin markers usually work better than thick markers or crayons.

Activity Three: The Mysteries of Pyramid Construction

Key Question: How were the pyramids built?

Focus Web Site

Mark Millmore's Ancient Egypt

Go to *http://www.teachercreated.com/books/2159*

Click on page 98, site 1

Companion Sites

Go to *http://www.teachercreated.com/books/2159*

Ancient Egypt	Click on page 98, site 2
Pyramid Construction	Click on page 98, site 3

Trips in Time: Ancient Egypt

Tell It Like It Was

http://www.teachercreated.com/books/2159   Click on page 98, sites 1-3

In this activity you're going to work with a team to write and produce a one-act play! The purpose of your play is to describe what life was like in ancient Egypt. You'll need to do some research before you can get started on the play, but once your research is done, it's playtime! Each person in your team will be assigned a certain role (queen, god, servant, etc.) for the play. Your job as a team is to write a script that shows life in ancient Egypt, using all those characters.

Key Question: What was life like in ancient Egypt?

Directions: Once you get your character assignment from your teacher, go to the Web sites above to find out about ancient Egypt. Use this page to collect your information. The better the research you do, the better your character will be! Once everyone is done with their research, get the team together to write a one-act, 10-minute play. Make sure the play shows what life was like for each of the characters in your team. If you want to, your play can center around a banquet table, a store, a meeting, a celebration, or anything else you can think of where all your characters might come together. When all the teams are ready, your class can put on a show – Egyptian style!

My role in the play: _____

My Research **General information about Ancient Egypt:**	**Information for my role:**
	Clothes my character might wear: Job my character might have: Things my character might have: Things my character might say: Something my character would never do:

©Teacher Created Resources, Inc.   99   #2159 Web Hunts and Virtual Field Trips

Trips in Time: Ancient Egypt

Picture Words

http://www.teachercreated.com/books/2159   Click on page 98, site 1

Key Question: How did ancient Egyptians communicate?

Directions: Go to the Ancient Egyptians Web site and click on the Hieroglyphs button. Use this site to write an advertisement for an ancient Egyptian newspaper. The ad can be for any of the following: (choose one)

  _____   I lost my favorite snake. He answers to the name "Viper."

  _____   I want to hire someone to decorate my pyramid.

  _____   I need to find a job. I'm an architect.

Once you've written your ad, post it on the wall where your teacher has told you to post your work. Once the class is finished, select one of the advertisements from the wall and respond to it (in Hieroglyphs of course). Deliver the response to the correct person and sit back and wait for the response to your ad!

Ready to get started? Use the space below to plan your advertisement.

I'm writing an ad for _____

My Advertisement

Title for my ad: _____

The ad: (limit—40-50 words)

_____

_____

_____

_____

_____

_____

Trips in Time: Ancient Egypt

The Mysteries of Pyramid Construction

http://www.teachercreated.com/books/2159   Click on page 98, site 3

The pyramids of Egypt were built many, many years ago, long before there were cranes and bulldozers and tractors. And yet, the pyramids were built out of huge blocks which weighed thousands of pounds each. How is it possible that an ancient people could have constructed these monuments without the tools we have today? This is a question which many great minds have pondered. And now – it's your turn!

Key Question: How were the pyramids built?

Directions: Without reading any of the information on pyramids, tell your theory of how the pyramids were built. Once you've written your theory, go to the Pyramid Construction Web site to find out if your theory is correct. After your visit to the pyramids, take notes on the theories you found on the Web site. Do you still think your theory was correct?

Building the Pyramids

My theory:

　　I think the pyramids were built using this plan…

_____

_____

_____

_____

_____

_____

The Web site theories:

　　According to the Web site, the pyramids were built…

_____

_____

_____

_____

_____

_____

_____

©Teacher Created Resources, Inc.　　　　　　　　　　#2159 Web Hunts and Virtual Field Trips

Trips in Time: The Freedom Trail

The Revolution Stroll

Background

Boston's Freedom Trail is a tangible chunk of history laid right at our feet. On this trip we'll create webs and charts to help us piece together the story of freedom!

Objectives

The student will create a web to represent nonfiction information.

The student will identify relationships between historic events and places.

The student will evaluate nonfiction text in order to find crucial information.

The Trip

Activity One: Webbing the Trail

Key Question: Can we turn the Freedom Trail into a giant web?

Materials: yarn, string, or pipe cleaners

Teacher Note: It's important to make sure that the center circle of each web is the main event or fact for the assigned stop on the Freedom Trail. The four outer circles of each web hold four supporting details about that main fact. Using plain white yarn or pipe cleaners is fine, but a fun modification to this activity is to have the class create a color code for the spokes of the web. Red pipe cleaners/yarn may stand for "…which lead to a battle…" or blue might stand for "…which made the people want to…"

Activity Two: Who? What? When? Where? Why?

Key Question: What are the important facts represented by the Freedom Trail?

Materials: 4X6 index cards (Lined on one side is better.)

Teacher Note: Once the cards are created, try using red yarn to lay the Freedom Trail out on your classroom floor! You might even want to build models of each of the stops on the trail. Use play-dough anchors to hold the index cards up near each stop.

Focus Web Site

National Park Service: The Freedom Trail

Go to *http://www.teachercreated.com/books/2159*

Click on page 102, site 1

Companion Sites

Go to *http://www.teachercreated.com/books/2159*

The Freedom Trail	Click on page 102, site 2
The City of Boston: The Freedom Trail	Click on page 102, site 3

Trips in Time: The Freedom Trail

Webbing the Trail

http://www.teachercreated.com/books/2159   Click on page 102, sites 1-3

Key Question: Can we turn the Freedom Trail into a giant web?

Directions: Use the Freedom Trail Web sites above to learn all you can about Boston's Freedom Trail. Once you're familiar with the facts, your teacher will assign you and a partner to create a web of one of the stops on the Freedom Trail. In the center circle, write the main fact, location or event for your stop on the trail. In the four support circles, write details that support or tell more about your center circle. Once all the webs are done, your class might want to try to combine them into one giant Freedom Trail web!

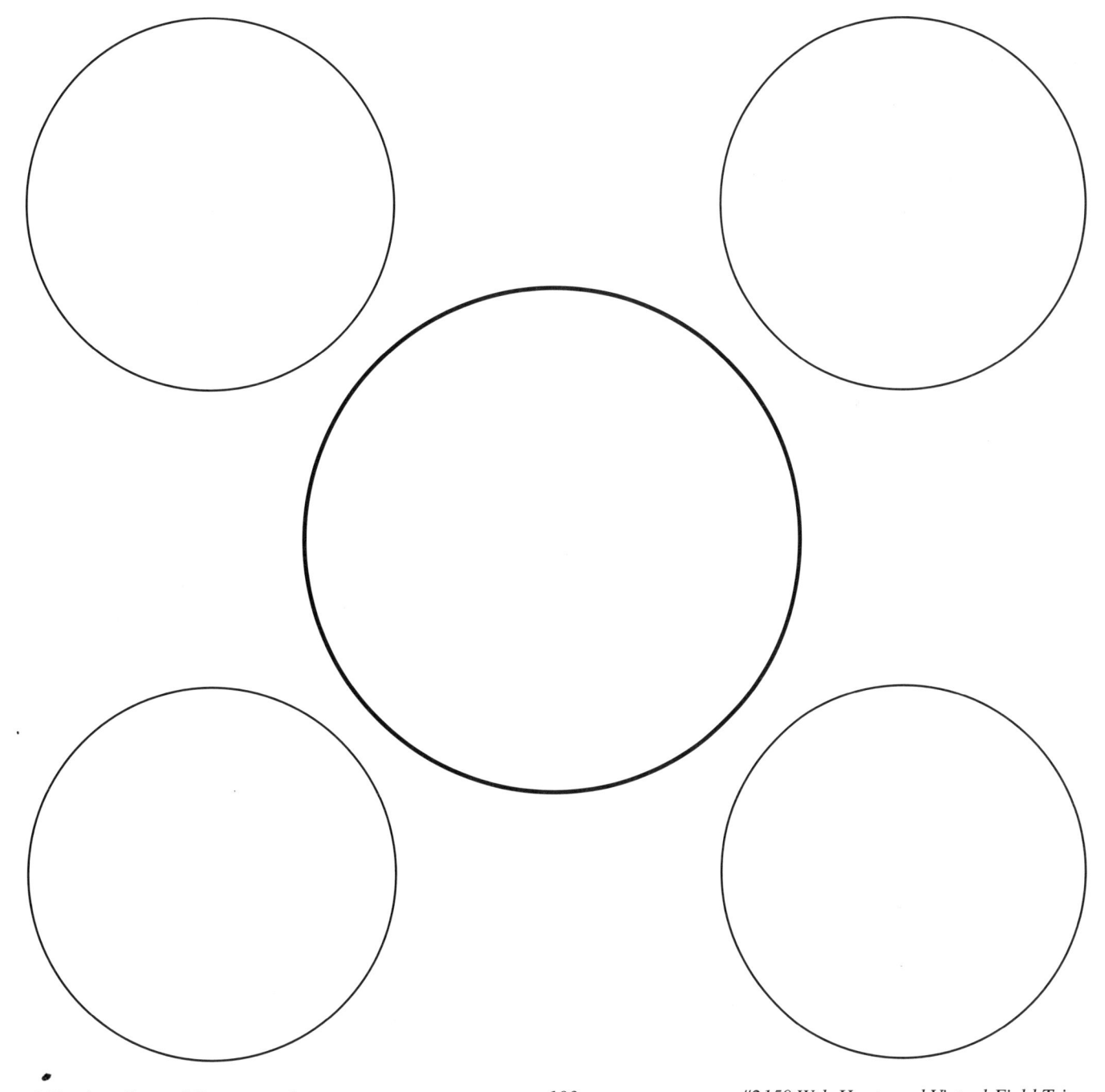

Trips in Time: The Freedom Trail

Who? What? When? Where? Why?

http://www.teachercreated.com/books/2159   Click on page 102, site 1

Key Question: What are the most important facts represented by the Freedom Trail?

Directions: Take this page with you as you hop on the Freedom Trail (the Web site, that is!). As you travel the trail, take some Skeleton Notes. Skeleton Notes are very brief, short notes. They have only the most crucial information in them. When you're done with your chart, your teacher will ask you and a partner to get together to compare charts. Once you've checked each other's charts, you'll be assigned one of the stops on the Freedom Trail. Create an index card which gives the information for your stop on the trail. Draw a picture of the stop on the front of the card (and give it a title too) and give all the Skeleton Facts for that stop on the back of the card. When you're done, turn it in to your teacher and get ready to build a trail!

Stop #	Stop Name	Who?	What?	When?	Where?	Why?

Trips in Time: The Renaissance

Lookin' Back with Leo!

Background

The Renaissance was one of the most fascinating times in history. So much new ground was being broken, especially in the sciences. One of the icons of this time is Leonardo da Vinci. By examining his life and work, we can better understand the Renaissance. Get ready for a little time travel!

Objectives

The student will read and synthesize nonfiction text from an online resource.

The student will complete a graphic organizer to demonstrate comprehension.

The student will draw correlations between the life of an eminent person and the era in which he lived.

The student will relate historical information to his/her own life.

The Trip

Activity One: Representative of the Renaissance
  Key Question: Who was Leonardo da Vinci, and what did he do?

Activity Two: Check Me Out!
  Key Question: What would my life have been like as a child during the Renaissance?
  Teacher Note: This site is very large. It's packed full of very interesting information, but it's too much information for most third to fifth graders, so you'll need to help get them to their site. From the main page, go through either Portal 1, 2 or 3 to get to the introduction. From there click on the link to "interesting characters," and on that page you'll find the link to William McVain, your host for this activity.

Focus Web Site

Leonardo's Workshop

  Go to *http://www.teachercreated.com/books/2159*

  Click on page 105, site 1

Companion Sites

  Go to *http://www.teachercreated.com/books/2159*

Exploring Leonardo	Click on page 105, site 2
Virtual Renaissance	Click on page 105, site 3
Renaissance Personalities Home Page (student project)	Click on page 105, site 4

©Teacher Created Resources, Inc.   #2159 Web Hunts and Virtual Field Trips

Trips in Time: The Renaissance

Representative of the Renaissance

http://www.teachercreated.com/books/2159   Click on page 105, sites 1-2

Key Question: Who was Leonardo da Vinci, and what did he do?

Directions: Take some time to really explore the Leonardo's Workshop Web site. You might want to spend some time on the Exploring Leonardo Web site as well. While you're there, or once you've returned, complete the web below by adding supporting facts from the Web sites.

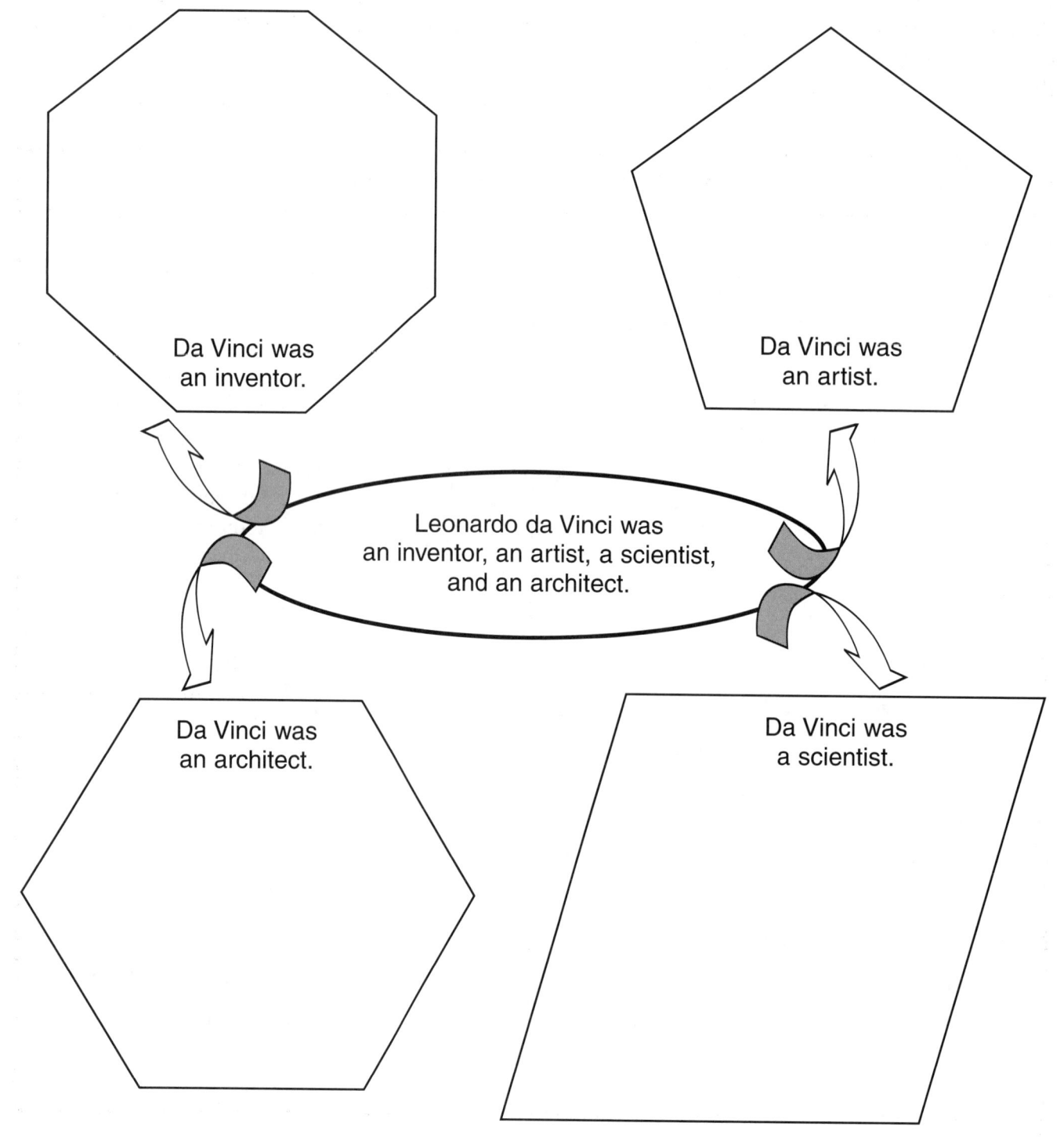

Da Vinci was an inventor.

Da Vinci was an artist.

Leonardo da Vinci was an inventor, an artist, a scientist, and an architect.

Da Vinci was an architect.

Da Vinci was a scientist.

Trips in Time: The Renaissance

Check Me Out!

http://www.teachercreated.com/books/2159   Click on page 105, site 3

Key Question: What would my life have been like as a child during the Renaissance?

Directions: Use the Virtual Renaissance Web site to complete this Renaissance task! You'll need to follow directions closely because you're going to meet someone who can help you with your chore. His name is William McVain, and you'll find him playing with a group of children by the river in the town. Your teacher will help you get through the town to get to William, but from then on, you're on your own. Listen to what William has to say about the life of kids in Renaissance times. Once you have your information, zoom back to the present so that you can complete this activity!

My Life as a Renaissance Kid	
What I'd look like	**Games I'd play**
	Chores I'd have

Trips in Space: Solar System

Sailing Around the Solar System

Background

The solar system is an enormous place full of incredible things to study. In this trip we'll be whirling around the stars as we travel from planet to planet in search of new information. Who knows? Maybe we'll even find an alien or two!

Objectives

The student will read and synthesize nonfiction text from an online resource.

The student will identify pressing questions and curiosities about the solar system.

The student will complete a research plan for the online exploration of a curiosity.

The student will extrapolate the characteristics of an environment into a fictional life form.

The Trip

Activity One: A Chart of Curiosities

Key Question: What makes me curious about outer space?

Activity Two: Research-O-Rama

Focus Point: Use the Internet for solar system research.

Activity Three: Who's Out There?

Key Question: What would aliens from different planets in our solar system look like?

Focus Web Site

Field Guide to the Universe

Go to *http://www.teachercreated.com/books/2159*

Click on page 108, site 1

Companion Sites

Go to *http://www.teachercreated.com/books/2159*

The Solar System	Click on page 108, site 2
The Space Place	Click on page 108, site 3
Solar System Simulator	Click on page 108, site 4
Space Day Brain Warp	Click on page 108, site 5
Why Files: Are We Alone?	Click on page 108, site 6
Discovery Online: Galaxy Tour	Click on page 108, site 7
Exploratorium: Build a Solar System	Click on page 108, site 8

Trips in Space: Solar System

A Chart of Curiosities

http://www.teachercreated.com/books/2159   Click on page 108, site 1

Key Question: What makes me curious about outer space?

Directions: Use the Field Guide to the Universe Web site to help you discover your own curiosities about the solar system. Take a quick tiptoe through the site. Don't stay too long; we just want to whet your appetite! Are you done yet? Hurry up! Don't stay long! Done now? Great! Now that you've seen a little bit of the solar system, it's time for you to create some questions! What are you curious about? What do you want to know more about? What puzzles you? Now is the time to jot down all those burning questions so that you can take charge of your own learning! Try to come up with three questions for each category below. Once you're done, circle the one you most want to know about!

I wonder if…

* ✳ _____
* ✳ _____
* ✳ _____

I want to know more about…

* ★ _____
* ★ _____
* ★ _____

I'm not sure about…

* ☞ _____
* ☞ _____
* ☞ _____

Freewheeling curiosities (so write any other questions that pop into your head):

* ❏ _____
* ❏ _____
* ❏ _____

Trips in Space: Solar System

Research-O-Rama

http://www.teachercreated.com/books/2159   Click on page 108, sites 1-8

Focus Point: Using the Internet for solar system research.

You chose an interesting topic in the previous activity. Now it's time to find the answer to your question! This paper is a research collection kit. It will help you find answers and discover new things – not to mention help keep you from getting lost out there in the solar system.

Step One: Stay Focused!

My question is _____

Step Two: Collect data that matches your topic.

Get a piece of lined notebook paper and make two columns on it. Label the columns like this:

Web Site Name	Information I Found There

Make several of these research pages if you think you might need them. Take them to the computer with you when you go online to the Solar System Web sites above. Travel through the sites collecting data in the form of notes. Don't stop until you get enough to cover your topic!

Step Three: Read the data you collected.

This step is fun. Pick a light-colored crayon or marker and get ready to rumble! With your crayon/marker in hand, read through all the information you collected and underline any information that very closely matches your topic or answers your question.

Step Four: Answer your question.

Doing the research isn't enough. You've got to write the answer to your question!

Use another sheet of paper to write the answer to your question in paragraphs.

Trips in Space: Solar System

Who's Out There?

http://www.teachercreated.com/books/2159   Click on page 108, site 1

Key Question: What would aliens from different planets in our solar system look like?

Directions: Use the Field Guide to the Universe Web site to get to know the planets in our solar system. Based on what you know about the planets, create an alien life form for one of the planets. Even though this is a creative exercise, you'll want to stay true to the characteristics of the planet. For example, you couldn't say that aliens on Mars have lungs and breathe oxygen because Mars doesn't have oxygen in its atmosphere. Use the planet to let you know what adaptations an alien would need in order to live there. Be sure to label the alien's features in the spaces provided!

The Planet: _____   **Alien's Name:** _____

What we Know about the planet	Picture of the Alien	Special features of your alien

Trips in Space: The Moon

Fly Me to the Moon

Background

The journey to the moon was a journey not just of science and technology but of the human spirit. These pages tell the sometimes forgotten, but always amazing, story of our first steps off Mother Earth. Where we go in the future comes directly from where we have been already and how we got there. Journey now into the past and out to the Moon.

Objectives

The student will read and synthesize nonfiction text from an online resource.

The student will organize information into a time line of events.

The student will use images to tell a story.

The student will demonstrate knowledge of historical information.

The student will rehearse the beginning, middle, and end qualities of a story.

The Trip

Activity One: Mapping the Journey

Key Question: What were the major events on the trip to the moon and back?

Activity Two: Cosmic Photo Albums

Key Question: How can photographs be used to tell a story?

Materials: You'll need to capture and print the images of the journey to the Moon from the Apollo 11 Web site. (Find step-by-step simple directions on page 143.)

Teacher Note: You may find this activity easier to do as a whole class. Adjust the difficulty level by adjusting the number of pictures used in this activity.

Focus Web Site

Apollo 11—30th Anniversary

Go to *http://www.teachercreated.com/books/2159*

Click on page 112, site 1

Companion Sites

Go to *http://www.teachercreated.com/books/2159*

The History Place: Apollo 11	Click on page 112, site 2
First Lunar Landing	Click on page 112, site 3
Historical Videos	Click on page 112, site 4

Trips in Space: The Moon

Mapping the Journey

http://www.teachercreated.com/books/2159   Click on page 112, sites 1-4

Key Question: What were the major events on the trip to the moon and back?

Directions: Read the Apollo 11 Web sites and get to know the details of our historic trip to the moon. Once you're done, try to fill in this pathway with the major events of the journey. Use arrows to show where on the trip the events happened!

©Teacher Created Resources, Inc.   113   #2159 Web Hunts and Virtual Field Trips

Trips in Space: The Moon

Name: _____ Date: _____

Cosmic Photo Albums

Key Question: How can photographs be used to tell a story?

Directions: Your teacher has printed out a set of photographs from the Apollo 11 trip to the moon. Now it's your turn to tell the story of the trip to the moon! Arrange the photographs so that they tell the story of the lunar expedition and then use your photo lineup to tell the story to the class!

Use the space below to jot down some notes for each photograph and then use this during your presentation.

Photo #	Details to Tell

Trips in Space: International Space Station

Living With the Stars

Background

The International Space Station is a monumental international effort which involves the construction of a permanent space station in Earth's orbit. On this trip we'll pop into the station to check it out! Who knows? Maybe one day we can really go up for a visit!

Objectives

The student will read and synthesize nonfiction text from an online resource.

The student will participate in a simulation which mimics life in space.

The student will recognize the dangers of space habitation.

The student will create components to add to an existing structure.

The Trip

Activity One: Station-Builders-R-Us

Key Question: What kind of module would you add to the space stations if you could?

Teacher Note: As a closing to this activity, you may want to have students create an evaluation grid (like the one on page 87) to evaluate the modules. Or you may want to have students bring in supplies so that they can each create a model of their ideas.

Activity Two: Space Life

Key Question: What would it be like to live in outer space?

Focus Web Sites

Space Station Blueprint

Space Station: Crew Bunk

Virtual Tour

NASA Kids

Go to *http://www.teachercreated.com/books/2159*

Click on page 115, sites 1, 2, 3, and 4

Companion Sites

Go to *http://www.teachercreated.com/books/2159*

Field Guide to the Universe: Spacecraft	Click on page 115, site 5
Cosmic Quest: Living in Space	Click on page 115, site 6
Time Line of Space Exploration	Click on page 115, site 7
Early Efforts in Space Exploration	Click on page 115, site 8

Trips in Space: International Space Station

Station-Builders-R-Us

http://www.teachercreated.com/books/2159   Click on page 115, sites 1-8

Key Question: What kind of module would you add to the space stations if you could?

Directions: Take some time to explore the space station on the Web sites provided above. Notice that the space station is constructed in a modular form. This means that the people who build it create individual sections which have special purposes. There's an area for sleeping, a kitchen, a laboratory, etc. Your job today is to create a new module. It can be anything you want – a game room, a photography room, a library, a computer room – the sky's the limit (literally). In the space below you need to draw a sketch of the outside and the inside of your module. Be sure to label all the important features and make sure you've dealt with the fact that you'll be living in zero gravity and will need to keep things from floating around!

My Space Station Module

Outside

Inside

Trips in Space: International Space Station

Space Life

http://www.teachercreated.com/books/2159   Click on page 115, site 6

Key Question: What would it be like to live in outer space?

Directions: Check out the Living in Space Web site and enjoy the simulation. While you're there, take some notes in the notes section of this page about the decisions you made and the results of your decisions. Once your simulation is over, turn the notes into a creative writing story about a "real" stay in the space station!

Simulation Notes

My Time On The Station

Trips to Nature: Rain Forest

Follow Me to the Woods!

Background

The rain forests are one of this planet's most beautiful and endangered resources. Thinking about taking your students to the rain forest? Better hurry this trip along before they're all gone!

Objectives

The student will read and synthesize nonfiction text from an online resource.
The student will identify plant, animal, and human inhabitants of the rain forest.
The student will recognize the diversity of life within the rain forest.
The student will appreciate the factors that threaten the rain forest.
The student will demonstrate comprehension of the levels of the rain forest.

The Trip

Activity One: A Trip Inside—Deep Inside!
Key Question: What lives inside the rain forest?

Activity Two: Threats to the Rain Forest
Key Question: What are the main threats to the health of the rain forest?

Activity Three: The Rain Forest - Right Here in My Bedroom!?
Key Question: What lives in each level of the rain forest and how is it similar to my habitat?

Focus Web Site

Overview of the Rain Forest (Rain Forest Education.com)
Go to *http://www.teachercreated.com/books/2159*
Click on page 118, site 1

Companion Sites

Go to *http://www.teachercreated.com/books/2159*

Rain Forest Education.com	Click on page 118, site 2
Rain Forests	Click on page 118, site 3
A Walk in the Rain Forest – A Self-Guided Tour	Click on page 118, site 4
Rain Forest Layers	Click on page 118, site 5
Rain Forest Activities	Click on page 118, site 6
Jason Project Archived Journey	Click on page 118, site 7

Trips to Nature: Rain Forest

A Trip Inside—Deep Inside!

http://www.teachercreated.com/books/2159 Click on page 118, sites 1-7

Key Question: What lives inside the rain forest?

Directions: Take this sheet with you when you go online to visit all the rain forest sites provided above. Make sure that you and your partner have your duties covered. Someone needs to navigate the mouse, and someone needs to record the evidence that you see, hear, and read. Take notes on every possible living thing you can, but make sure you put them in the correct categories. When you're done, go over your work together and get ready to use your notes to help fill in a class chart.

Plants	Animals	Humans

Trips to Nature: Rain Forest

Threats to the Rain Forest

http://www.teachercreated.com/books/2159   Click on page 118, sites 1-7

Key Question: What are the main threats to the health of the rain forest?

Directions: Use the Rain Forest sites above to help you to identify at least three threats to the rain forest. Use the information you find to fill in this chart. For every threat there is a cause and a correction. Your job is to try to figure out what (or who) the cause is for each threat. You must also discover the best cure for each threat you find. Good luck! Keep your eyes open for information – it could be hiding anywhere!

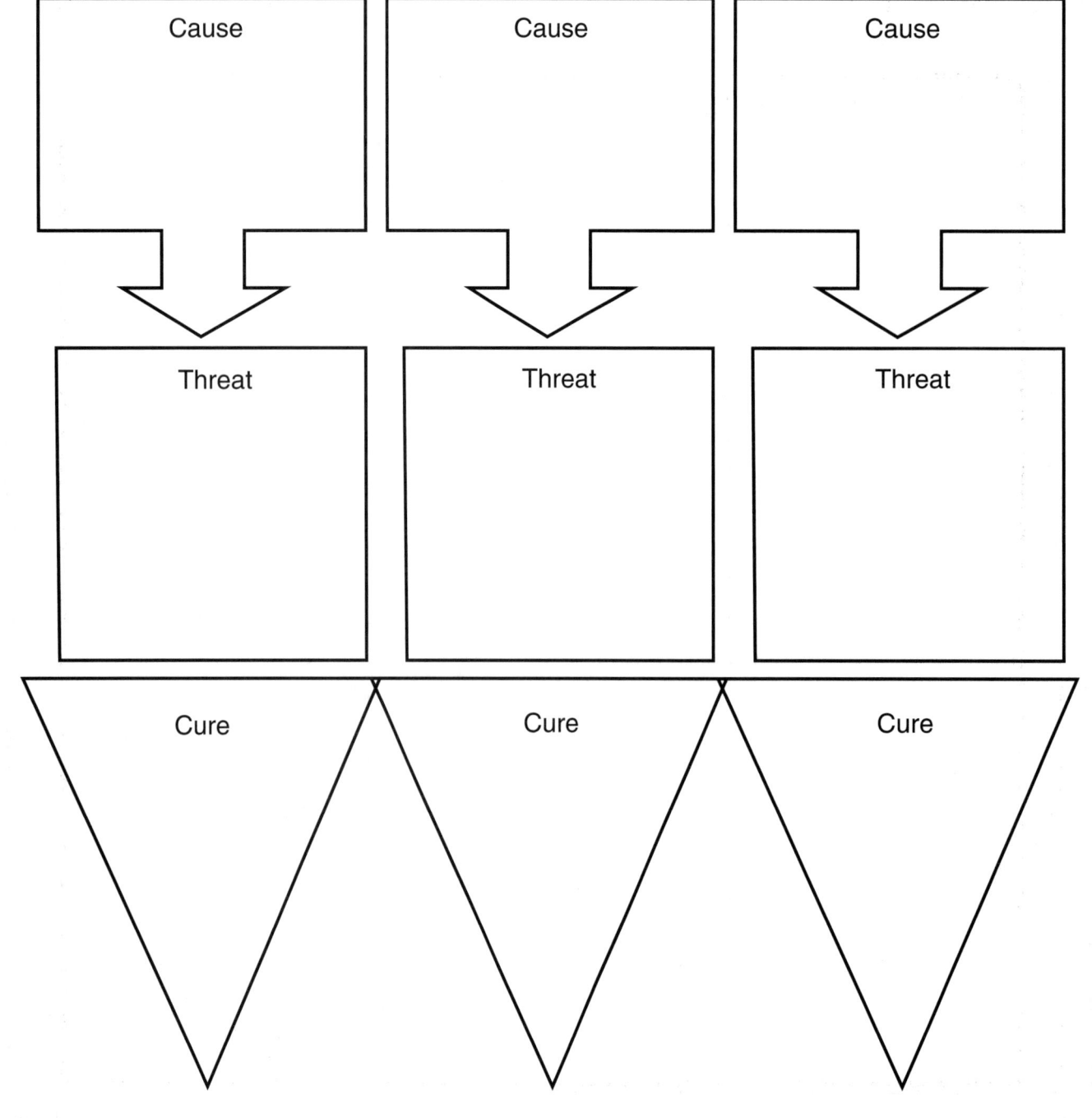

Cause	Cause	Cause
↓	↓	↓
Threat	Threat	Threat
Cure	Cure	Cure

Trips to Nature: Rain Forest

The Rain Forest - Right Here in My Bedroom!?

http://www.teachercreated.com/books/2159   Click on page 118, site 5

Key Question: What lives in each level of the rain forest and is it similar to my habitat?

Directions: Use the Rain Forest Layers Web site to help you with this activity. On the left side of this page, draw a picture which represents a cross-section of the layers of the rain forest. Be sure that you represent all the plants living in each layer. On the right side of the page, draw a similar picture, but this time draw your bedroom! What is found in each layer of YOUR habitat? Do you see any similarities between a rain forest and your bedroom?

The Rain Forest	My Room

©Teacher Created Resources, Inc.   121   #2159 Web Hunts and Virtual Field Trips

Trips to Nature: Galapagos Islands

To a Place Like No Other

Background

The Galapagos Islands have long been a source of interest for researchers, conservationists, biologist, botanists, and more. With such a unique landscape, it is a compelling sight. The varied animals living on and near these islands make it an interesting area to visit and study. Today we launch our boats into the water to venture to the Galapagos!

Objectives

The student will read and synthesize nonfiction text from an online resource.

The student will write a first-person account of a geological discovery.

The student will incorporate details in his/her writing.

The student will harvest information from an online source.

The student will create questions and answers out of facts/information.

The Trip

Activity One: Dear Diary, I Found an Island Today…
　Key Question: What might the first person to discover the Galapagos have written in his diary?

Activity Two: Put on Your Game Face!
　Key Question: Can we pass our knowledge on to others through games?

Focus Web Sites

Destination: Galapagos Islands

World Wildlife Fund (WWF): The Galapagos

WWF: Slide Show

　Go to *http://www.teachercreated.com/books/2159*

　Click on page 122, sites 1, 2, 3

Companion Sites

　Go to *http://www.teachercreated.com/books/2159*

Map of the Galapagos　　　　　　　　　　　　　　Click on page 122, site 4

Trips to Nature: Galapagos Islands

Dear Diary, I Found an Island Today...

http://www.teachercreated.com/books/2159   Click on page 122, sites 1-4

The Galapagos Islands were discovered by Fray Tomas de Berlanga in 1535 when he bumped into them while sailing from Panama to Peru*. These islands were probably unlike anything seen before. They had a unique habitat and an incredible variety of inhabitants. The discoverer must have discovered that this was an incredible place indeed.

*See the PBS companion site for more details on visitors to the islands.

Key Question: What might the first person to discover the Galapagos have written in his diary?

Directions: Use the Galapagos Islands Web sites to learn all you can about the islands and their inhabitants. Once you're familiar with the islands, create a diary entry that shows how an early explorer would have felt upon approaching the island. What would he have seen when he explored them. What would he have thought and felt? What would he have done? How did he come up with the names for each island? What did he think of all the strange animals? Use details from the Web sites to make your diary believable.

March 10, 1535

Dear Diary,

Today I found an island...

Trips to Nature: Galapagos Islands

Put on Your Game Face!

http://www.teachercreated.com/books/2159   Click on page 122, sites 1-4

Key Question: Can we pass on our knowledge to others through games?

Directions: Use the Galapagos Islands Web sites to collect information for this activity. Your class is going to create a Jeopardy! game in order to pass on knowledge about the Galapagos Islands. The game is pretty easy to create; the research phase is the most important part of the process. Your teacher has given you an assignment to collect two facts in the following categories: Life, Geology, Exploration, Galapagos Today, and Conservation. That's just ten facts total! The tricky part is that you have to decide if your facts are too easy, too hard, or just right for your difficulty level. (Your teacher will tell you what difficulty level you get to do.) Once you've got your assignment and your partner, start collecting your facts below.

Difficulty Level: (circle one)   1   2   3   4   5

Life	Geology	Exploration	Galapagos Today	Conservation

Once you're finished, turn each fact in your chart into a question and answer pairing for the Jeopardy! game. Write each one on a separate index card. Be sure to write the category on the front of the card. Turn them in to your teacher when you're ready.

Trips to Nature: The Desert

An Ocean of Sand—But That's Not All

Background

What do most students think of when they think of the desert? Right—sand. This is their chance to learn about the varied inhabitants of America's deserts. On this trip we'll not only look at the desert's ecosystem, but we'll also take a look at the animals who call the desert home.

Objectives

The student will read and synthesize nonfiction text from an online resource.
The student will recognize that desert ecosystems can and do support life.
The student will record and organize data from a Web site.
The student will identify adaptation features of desert dwelling animals.

The Trip

Activity One: At First Glance

Key Question: What do we think of when we think of the desert?

Materials: Use the procedure on page 143 to print out two sets of pictures of deserts. The first set should be stereotypical desert scenery (dry, hot, no life, sand). The second set should show the various inhabitants of the desert, the colors of the desert, and should break the stereotype supported in the first set.

Activity Two: Life in the Desert

Key Question: Are desert animals special?

Focus Web Site

The Chihuahuan Desert Region
Go to *http://www.teachercreated.com/books/2159*
Click on page 125, site 1

Companion Sites

Go to *http://www.teachercreated.com/books/2159*

Desert Animal Printouts	Click on page 125, site 2
North American Deserts	Click on page 125, site 3
Desert Botanical Gardens (student project)	Click on page 125, site 4
Sahara Crosser's Corner	Click on page 125, site 5
The John S. Park Desert Art Gallery	Click on page 125, site 6
Petrified Forest National Park – Photographs	Click on page 125, site 7
Bitsti Badlands – Phtographs	Click on page 125, site 8
Bryce Canyon National Park – Photographs	Click on page 125, site 9

Trips to Nature: The Desert

At First Glance

http://www.teachercreated.com/books/2159   Click on page 125, sites 4, 6-9

Key Question: What do we think of when we think of the desert?

Directions:

1. In the rectangle below, write down as many words as you can think of to describe a desert. Don't hold back. Use colors, textures, sounds, smells, sights, etc.

2. Take a look at the pictures on sites 4, 6, 7, 8 and 9.

3. In the octagon below, make a new list of words to describe a desert. Don't use any words from the rectangle; *use all new words*.

4. Write a short answer to the questions on the bottom part of this page.

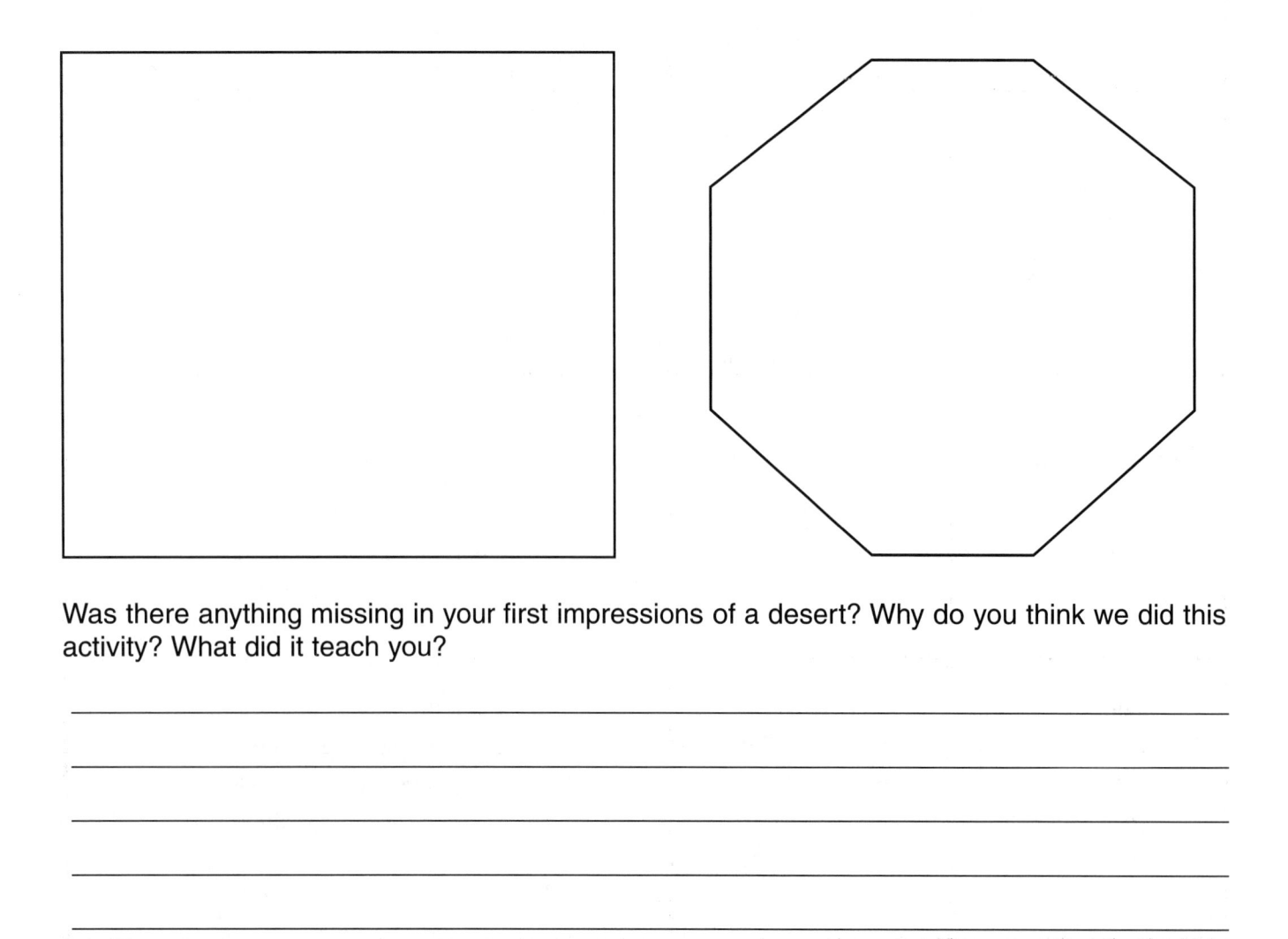

Was there anything missing in your first impressions of a desert? Why do you think we did this activity? What did it teach you?

_____
_____
_____
_____

Trips to Nature: The Desert

Life in the Desert

http://www.teachercreated.com/books/2159   Click on page 125, sites 1-2

Key Question: Are desert animals special?

Directions: Use the Desert Web sites provided to learn more about the animals of the desert. You may have to do a little investigative research – look for clues and evidence – because the answers for the chart below might not be obvious! Choose any four desert animals and complete the chart.

The Animal	Quick Sketch	Adaptations/Characteristics for Desert Life

Trips to Famous Places: Stonehenge

Play Blocks for Giants

Background

Stonehenge has been a source of study for so many different kinds of people – from mystics to astronomers, from meteorologists to architects. It seems like everyone is interested in the mysteries of Stonehenge, so why not get our students interested too? Pack your bags and bring an extra case of curiosity because we're heading to England!

Objectives

The student will develop a plausible theory and an implausible theory to explain the same event.

The student will recognize the existence of modern-day mysteries.

The student will formulate theories on the construction of Stonehenge.

The student will present and defend the theories before a group of peers.

The Trip

Activity One: All Right, Who Left Their Toys on the Lawn?
   Key Question: What is Stonehenge?

Activity Two: Rock and Roll
   Key Question: How was Stonehenge built?

Focus Web Sites

Stonehenge: Photograph 1

Stonehenge: Photograph 2

   Go to *http://www.teachercreated.com/books/2159*

   Click on page 128, sites 1 & 2

Companion Sites

   Go to *http://www.teachercreated.com/books/2159*

Stonehenge (1)	Click on page 128, site 3
Stonehenge (2)	Click on page 128, site 4
Stonehenge: Phases of Construction	Click on page 128, site 5
Mystic Places Tour	Click on page 128, site 6
Stonehenge: Teacher Resource	Click on page 128, site 7

Trips to Famous Places: Stonehenge

All Right, Who Left Their Toys on the Lawn?

http://www.teachercreated.com/books/2159   Click on page 128, sites 1-2

Key Question: What is Stonehenge?

Directions: Take a look at the photographs on the Web sites provided. Study them both and pay attention to the details of each picture. Once you've studied the pictures, think about what you saw and make a decision about what it is. You may already know that the pictures are of a place called Stonehenge. The question is – what is it? It sits in the middle of a field in England, but why? What is it for? What was it for? Theories about Stonehenge claim that it was a calendar, a timekeeper, a tool to read the stars, or even an altar. While these are all possibilities, no one is exactly sure what Stonehenge's original purpose was!

Now it's your turn to try to solve the mystery of Stonehenge. You need to create two theories – one that is plausible (possible, something that "could be") and one that is strictly implausible (fantasy, "no way, couldn't be").

Could Be!	No Way!
What makes this theory possible?	**What makes this theory impossible?**

©Teacher Created Resources, Inc.   129   #2159 Web Hunts and Virtual Field Trips

Trips to Famous Places: Stonehenge

Rock and Roll

http://www.teachercreated.com/books/2159   Click on page 128, sites 1-6

Key Question: How was Stonehenge built?

Directions: It's theory time again! This time you need to pretend to be the creator of Stonehenge. You're a builder living in 2800 B.C. You heard about a new project in the area, and you want to be in charge of the job. There are many builders who want to be chosen, and the one who turns in the best plans will win. The design of the structure has already been decided (check the Web sites for details), so there's no need to draw blueprints for the construction. The trick to this job will be in the actual building itself. Each builder will have to answer the question: How will we move the huge stones to the site and into position? The answer to this question can win you this important job.

In the space below write a letter to the head of the Stonehenge Council and explain to her your reasons for wanting the job and how you plan to solve the pressing question. Remember, other builders are vying for this dream job, so make sure you've got all the answers!

TO: Madame Rocks TuHeavy
     President of the Stonehenge Council

FROM: _____
      Master Builder

RE: Upcoming Job at Stonehenge

Dear Madam President,

Please allow me to introduce myself. My name is _____, and I am a master builder living in southern England. I heard recently that you are looking for a builder to build a structure called Stonehenge…

_____
_____
_____
_____
_____
_____
_____
_____

Trips to Famous Places: Mount Rushmore

Facing the Test of Time

Background

Mount Rushmore is such an awesome sight – those four strong, hard faces chiseled forever into stone. Unlike Stonehenge, we know exactly why this monument is here, though some of us don't know exactly why these four men were chosen. In this trip to the mountains of South Dakota, we'll find out a little bit more about this wonderful place. We'll also let Rushmore call us into our nation's past to help us to find out more about these four famous faces.

Objectives

The student will read and synthesize nonfiction text from an online resource.

The student will conduct online research about former presidents.

The student will evaluate the rationale behind the Rushmore selection process in order to determine agreement or disagreement.

The student will evaluate current personalities and leaders.

The Trip

Activity One: These Guys Rock!

Key Question: Why were Washington, Lincoln, Roosevelt, and Jefferson chosen to be the faces of Mount Rushmore?

Teacher Note: A fun follow-up activity is to ask your students how aliens looking at Earth from outer space might try to explain Mount Rushmore. What might the aliens be thinking about our glorious mountain? They might think the mountain is a tomb. Let your class exhaust the possibilities! Another idea is to question the lack of a woman's face on the mountain. What woman of that day might have been placed on the mountain?

Activity Two: Who Should Get a Whole Mountain?

Key Question: Which of today's personalities or leaders would be picked for a current Mount Rushmore?

Focus Web Sites

Mount Rushmore: Creation
Mount Rushmore: History
   Go to *http://www.teachercreated.com/books/2159*
   Click on page 131, sites 1 & 2

Companion Sites

   Go to *http://www.teachercreated.com/books/2159*

Mount Rushmore: Photographs	Click on page 131, site 3
Mount Rushmore	Click on page 131, site 4
Presidents of the United States	Click on page 131, site 5

©Teacher Created Resources, Inc.   #2159 Web Hunts and Virtual Field Trips

Trips to Famous Places: Mount Rushmore

These Guys Rock!

http://www.teachercreated.com/books/2159   Click on page 131, sites 1-5

Key Question: Why were Washington, Lincoln, Roosevelt, and Jefferson chosen to be the faces of Mount Rushmore?

Directions: Use the Mount Rushmore Web sites and the White House Web site on the presidents to help you to decide why each of these four men was chosen to be immortalized on Mount Rushmore. Then move over to the right-hand side and let us know if you agree or disagree with the choice – and why!

The Presidents	Why was this man chosen?	Do you agree or disagree?	Why? Explain your answer.

Trips to Famous Places: Mount Rushmore

Name: _____ Date: _____

Who Should Get a Whole Mountain?

Key Question: Which of today's personalities or leaders would be picked for a current Mount Rushmore?

Directions: Help the class brainstorm a list of personalities and leaders on the board. Anything goes; try to fill up the whole board! Once your class list is done, choose four faces you want to put on your mountain! Once you've decided on your four faces, draw a picture of your Mt. Rushmore! Below each face explain why you chose that person for your mountain.

My Mt. Rushmore

Who _____	Who _____	Who _____	Who _____
Why I chose:	Why I chose:	Why I chose:	Why I chose:

©Teacher Created Resources, Inc. #2159 Web Hunts and Virtual Field Trips

Trips to Famous Places: The Great Wall of China

Fences Make Good Neighbors... But This Is a Bit Much

Background

The Great Wall of China is an architectural and engineering feat. In this trip to China we'll learn more about the practical and beautiful symbol of power. This is a short trip, so make sure you don't miss a minute!

Objectives

The student will read and synthesize nonfiction text from an online resource.

The student will explore the structure and purpose of the Great Wall of China.

The student will extrapolate knowledge of the Great Wall of China into the use of walls in America.

The Trip

Activity One: Here a Wall, There a Wall, Everywhere a Wall, Wall

Key Question: Do Americans use many walls? What for and why?

Teacher Note: A neat extension for this activity would be to take a road map of the United States and stand a paver (thin) brick on the map (try separating strategic locations or blockading major transport roads). You might want to try this with a city or county map too. Discuss the effects/results of such divisions in the United States.

Focus Web Site

The Great Wall

Go to *http://www.teachercreated.com/books/2159*

Click on page 134, site 1

Companion Sites

Go to *http://www.teachercreated.com/books/2159*

The Great Wall of China	Click on page 134, site 2
A Map of The Great Wall	Click on page 134, site 3
The Great Wall: (teacher resource)	Click on page 134, site 4

Name: _____ Date: _____

Here a Wall, There a Wall, Everywhere a Wall, Wall

Key Question: Do Americans use many walls? What for and why?

Directions: After learning about the Great Wall of China with your class, learn about the walls in your neighborhood. Take this paper with you on your walk or ride home today and take notes on any walls that you see. Jot down as many details as you can before you pass them. Bring this paper back to school on _____ (date) so that the whole class can compare their findings. On the back, write your answer to the Key Question!

#	Type of wall or fence (wood, brick, stone, etc.)	Location (yard, lot, etc.)	Why is it there? (estimate) (decoration, pets, safety, etc.)

Appendix

Creating Your Own Web Hunts & Virtual Field Trips . 137 - 139

Our Internet Rules 140

A Classroom Poster of Our Internet Rules 141

Internet Research Road Map 142

Directions for Getting Graphics off the Internet 143

Glossary 144

Appendix

Creating Your Own Web Hunts & Virtual Field Trips

When you're ready to start creating your own Web hunts and virtual field trips, there are a few things you'll want to keep in mind to make the process run smoothly.

1. Always start with the curriculum first.

    Whether you're building a Web hunt or a virtual field trip, you'll want to be sure that you start with the curriculum as your focus. Being clear about your learning objectives is the best way to create a sound educational tool.

2. Make decisions about what you're going to search for BEFORE you start searching.

    Using search engines can be a very frustrating process. It is easy to get lost or to travel too far down a "side street" which leads nowhere. Become familiar with a few of the many search engines and Web site collections before you begin a serious or time-intensive search. We have a collection of search engines which you might find helpful. (Go to *http://www.teachercreated.com/books/2159* and Click on page 76.) One of the best things you can do is to visit the "Help" sections of the search engine sites. They provide valuable information about how to use each specific search engine.

3. Collect more sites than you think you'll need.

    Plan on collecting about two times as many sites as you're planning to use in your actual activity. That way you'll have sites to fall back on if they go down either temporarily or permanently. It's also nice to have extras because then you'll have lots of options, and you can pick the best sites to match your objectives.

4. Examine the sites from a student's perspective.

    One of the most important things to consider when evaluating Web sites for student use is readability. Is the content of the site on a reading level that matches your students' needs? Look for other things, too, like excess information, over abundance of "eye candy" (unnecessary graphics), confusing layout, or inappropriate advertising.

5. Construct activity pages to go along with each activity.

    Remember that your students are going online to collect or review information (Web hunts) or to explore and get to know information (virtual field trips). Either way, they'll need a place to take notes, collect data, or construct learning, so give them some organizational tools to help them stay on task!

Appendix

Building Hunts and Trips Work Sheet

Content Area: _____ **Grade Level:** _____

Learning objectives/benchmarks I want to support:

1. _____
2. _____
3. _____

Search words to use when searching for sites:

Web Site Collection

URL	Quick Description
_____	_____
_____	_____
_____	_____
_____	_____
_____	_____
_____	_____
_____	_____
_____	_____

Appendix

Appendix

Building Hunts and Trips Work Sheet (cont.)

Now that I've collected all the sites I think I might use, it's time to narrow down my focus to just a few of the sites and to build activities to go along with them. The best way to construct an activity is to focus on what my students can actively do either collecting data or using data in another activity. It is helpful to decide if the site is best for **information collection (IC)** or for an **activity (A)**.

Web site   IC/A

_____   _____

What can my kids DO on this site?

1. _____
2. _____

Web site   IC/A

_____   _____

What can my kids DO on this site?

1. _____
2. _____

Web site   IC/A

_____   _____

What can my kids DO on this site?

1. _____
2. _____

Web site   IC/A

_____   _____

What can my kids DO on this site?

1. _____
2. _____

©Teacher Created Resources, Inc.   #2159 Web Hunts and Virtual Field Trips

Appendix

Our Internet Rules

The Internet is a special tool that can help me learn, communicate and solve problems. Before I can use the Internet at my school, there are some promises that I need to make to my teacher, my classmates, my parents and myself. These promises are made to help keep me safe and to make my time on the Internet fun, interesting and educational.

When I use the Internet, I promise to . . .

. . . treat the people I "meet" on the Internet and the machines I use with respect.

. . . act as a representative of my school, showing everyone that I can act responsibly.

. . . tell my teacher or another adult when I see or my group sees something which is inappropriate or makes me feel uncomfortable.

. . . follow all of the instructions my teacher gives and stay only in the areas he/she suggests to me.

. . . actively use the information I find on the Internet in my learning (projects, reports, discussions).

. . . use the Internet as a learning tool to help me discover my world. I should know WHY I'm using the Internet for a certain task.

. . . share the activities I do on the Internet at home. It's important to let Mom and Dad know what I'm doing on the Internet and why I'm there.

. . . be aware that there are consequences for choosing not to follow the Internet rules.

I understand that my teacher knows how to keep me safe on the Internet, so it's important for me to follow directions. I understand that there are some things on the Internet that are not meant for children. If I find anything on the Internet that makes me feel uncomfortable, I know it's important to share that with my teacher right away.

Student Signature:_____   Teacher Signature: _____

Parent Signature:_____   Principal Signature: _____

© 1997 Internet Mentors Field Guide, Orange County Public Schools
Reprinted with permission from the author, Deirdre Kelly dkelly@magicnet.net

We're Responsible Users!

When I use the Internet, I promise to...

... treat the people I "meet" on the Internet and the machines I use with respect.

... act as a representative of my school, showing everyone that I can act responsibly.

... tell my teacher or another adult when I see or my group sees something which is inappropriate or makes me feel uncomfortable.

... follow all of the instructions my teacher gives and stay only in the areas he/she suggests to me.

... actively use the information I find on the Internet in my learning (projects, reports, discussions).

... use the Internet as a learning tool to help me discover my world. I should know WHY I'm using the Internet for a certain task.

... share the activities I do on the Internet at home. It's important to let Mom and Dad know what I'm doing on the Internet and why I'm there.

... be aware that there are consequences for choosing not to follow the Internet rules.

© *1997 Internet Mentors Field Guide, Orange County Public Schools*
Reprinted with permission from the author, Deirdre Kelly dkelly@magicnet.net

Appendix

Internet Research Road Map

I need to find...   (Be specific!)

My plan for finding it is...

☐   I have permission to use search engines for the information I need to find. I'm going to run searches on these words:

☐   I don't have permission to use search engines, but my teacher suggested that I research on these Web sites.

Site(s) I can visit: 1. _____

2. _____

Time I started: _____   Time I'm allowed online: _____   Time stopped: _____

The results of my search...(Be sure to take notes on what you find! Use the back of this page too!)

© 1997 Internet Mentors Field Guide, Orange County Public Schools
Reprinted with permission from author, Deirdre Kelly dkelly@magicnet.net

#2159 Web Hunts and Virtual Field Trips ©Teacher Created Resources, Inc.